Random

A novel by

Charong Chow

Copyright © 2011 by Charong Chow

All rights reserved

First Edition, 2011

The publishers have made every effort to identify the copyright

holders of the quoted material, where they have been unsuccessful

they invite the copyright holder to contact Charong Chow directly at:

me@charong.com.

Cover photo by Charong Chow

Cover designed by Nancy Choe

www.charong.com

To Jeremy,

Paradise, Hudson and Alexander

1

I knew he would be desperate to meet me. As I approach from Pacific Coast Highway, a crescent moon frowns over the glow of the Ferris Wheel and other amusements on the pier. Tom is standing outside his truck, as I park my mom's car.

He lays out his pleas against our breakup as we walk past the rides.

"We're too good together. You're not the type to listen to what others say. I was angry when I said those things. I never meant them. I've never loved anyone like you before, even if I am only seventeen."

I nod without much beyond my poker face. He stops walking and faces me.

"Are you going to say anything to me?"

"Can we have a hug?" I ask, causing a tender smile to break across his face.

He immediately clasps his long arms around me, almost taking my breath away. I hope for an emotional sense of anything. I feel nothing, no sadness, no happiness. He understands he doesn't have a girlfriend anymore.

"Why did you ask me to meet you here?" he says.

"I don't know. Maybe I wanted to know if it was really over."

"I don't want it to be, Tierney."

I walk to the end of the pier past the Mexican restaurant and a lone fisherman gazing at the crashing waves. Tom follows silently. It's dark and deserted. I walk down the farthest deck, three steps below the rest of the pier.

"My dad used to bring me here all the time when I was a girl," I start. "We tried fishing a few times... I know this place like the back of my hand."

"Catch anything?" Tom asks.

"No, just some seaweed once," I reply.

"It's nice here."

"Maybe I wanted closure?" I say, looking over at him. I put my arms on the railing just above the rough murky water.

"I'm sorry," he says.

"For what?" I ask, with an intense look.

"I don't know. That it turned out this way."

"The moon looks beautiful tonight," I say, pointing up.

"It's not as beautiful as you, you're glowing in it's light," Tom says to me.

"When I was little, I would call that kind of moon a banana moon. My parents thought that was so cute."

His dark brown eyes look pitiful and sad, full of desire and longing, completely opposite to when we first met on that fateful morning, his first day of school.

***

I remember that Friday. My mom saw Jeremy's fancy birthday present when she dropped me off. We had just arrived at school as Jeremy was getting out of his new red Audi station wagon.

"Mom, stop over there, to the right. I see Jeremy."

"Great car he has there."

"He just got it for his sixteenth birthday from his dad."

"Nice dad."

She stopped the car and I jumped out with my school things.

"Yeah, but he's never here for him. He didn't even give the car to him. He had the dealership drop it off at J's mom's place with a big red ribbon. Bye"

"Bye, dear."

I walked over to Jeremy, who immediately smiled.

"Hey there!"

"Hello, I need to ask you something."

"Whether or not we should bail today?" Jeremy laughed.

"No, not today, we have a math test."

"When did that ever stop you?"

I gave him my disapproving look. "I was going to ask what have we been doing in class lately?"

"Yes, Miss Tierney, I'll give you some notes."

We walked towards school, watching a black pickup truck pull up to the student parking lot. Jeremy pulled me back, and I stopped in my tracks. Then I saw him.

"Is he new?" I whispered to Jeremy.

"I don't know," Jeremy said, staring just as intently as I was. "We should ask him. Let's go."

"No, I don't…"

But it was too late. Jeremy walked right over to him. The new boy's chocolate brown hair and guilty smile seemed to beckon me. He was wearing the uniform of all the guys I knew, cargo pants, Undefeated T-shirt, and a black hoodie. He had a strong build that looked as if it would be good at any sport, if he cared. The features in his face changed from every angle, but he was definitely someone you could spend your days dreaming about. Jeremy, of course, practically drooled as we approached.

"Hey, there. New to school?"

"Yes, actually I am."

Standing behind Jeremy, I was embarrassed and somehow intimidated by this stranger. I didn't fully understand our destiny yet. He looked at me, almost reading my mind.

"I don't bite," he said, smiling. "I'm Tom."

Jeremy cut in, "Well Tom, I'm Jeremy and this is Tierney."

"What's your name again?" Tom asked me, obviously puzzled.

"It's Tierney... I'm named after Gene Tierney," I said.

"The Hollywood actress?" he asked.

"Yeah, my parents were fans."

"It's nice. I like that."

"Thanks."

We were standing there...and Jeremy busted out: "We're thinking of ditching today. Wanna come?"

"We can't, Jeremy. We have a math test, remember?" I reminded him.

"It doesn't matter. We can make it up."

"Well, it is my first day," Tom said. "Maybe I should go to school today."

"Okay, you are both goody-goodies," Jeremy pouted. "We'll stay."

I laughed and pulled Jeremy to the main building, wanting our conversation to end. Tom followed us, causing Jeremy to continue with the twenty questions.

"Where did you come from?" he began.

"New York."

"East Coast, huh?" Jeremy chuckled.

"My parents got divorced and my mom's from here. So we moved to my grandparents' house," explained Tom.

As we approached the main door and all the other plebs at school, Maya dashed out. She grabbed Jeremy's and my arms.

"Come on, let's get out of here."

"What's the hurry?" I asked.

"It's Friday, why does there have to be a reason?" she replied.

Tom reluctantly waved goodbye, not really understanding what was going on. Jeremy stopped Maya and curled his finger at Tom with a come-hither gesture.

"You're coming with us. No choice in the matter."

"Who's this?" asked Maya. "J's new boyfriend?"

Tom looked affronted. "Maybe," smiled Jeremy.

"No," said Tom, a little too sharply.

"Let's go before anyone sees us," I told them all firmly.

***

We returned to the student parking lot. When we saw Jeremy's car, we ran towards it laughing.

"Shotgun," screamed Maya, as she sat in the front passenger seat. Tom and I took the back seat. As Jeremy started his engine, Maya turned to Tom and me.

"Okay, so I saw Christy, that dumb blond cheerleader chick, wearing silver Uggs today."

"That's why we're bailing?" I exclaimed.

"Why is she wearing them?"

"Because you've had them for about a month already, and you're cool and she's not," I said.

She grinned.

"I told you those things were over. Don't wear them anymore."

"Maybe you're right."

I turned to Tom. "Is this how it is in New York?"

"I was at an all boys' school with uniforms."

Jeremy looked through his rear view mirror. "I love a man in uniform." We all laughed.

"Who are you?" asked Maya.

"He's the new guy," Jeremy said. "We found him in the parking lot."

"Like a stray dog?" Maya asked.

"Something like that," said Jeremy.

"Sorry, they're always this annoying. Sometimes I don't know why I hang out with them," I told Tom.

"It's not annoying me," he said. "This is fun."

"Oh, damn," Jeremy shouted. He looked serious. "Bosco is out of town this weekend."

"Don't worry, I can call English Dave," I told Jeremy calmly. "But it's a little early."

"Perfect. We have to show Tom here a good time."

"It's my talent, one of my many skills," I said to Tom.

"What's your talent?" he asked, with smile.

He knew, but he wanted me to say it out loud.

"I can score anywhere in the world."

"I am sure you can."

"Last year in Tokyo, with Jeremy, we found plenty of fun from some Dutch guy. It was really expensive, but I met some people at this club..."

"So this is the kind of fun we're going to have today?"

"Is that okay?" I smiled.

"Don't act all innocent, Tom," yelled Jeremy.

"I'll manage," Tom said.

***

I look at him now on the pier.

"Can I ask you something?" I say. "Why did you do it?"

"What?"

"All those bad things?"

"I don't know what you're talking about," Tom says, with a glimmer in his eyes that scares me.

"I know about New York, and…" I can't stop the tears. "I know what you did to my best friend!"

2

Growing up as latch key kids, we were pros at the perfect

mac and cheese and entertaining ourselves. J's house was always

empty since his parent's divorce, so we usually congregated there.

When we pulled up outside that first day with Tom, Jeremy turned

to him.

"Mom's at her boyfriend's this weekend. Be glad we don't

have to look at his middle-aged naked bum!"

"You would love that," screamed Maya.

We all laughed hysterically. I was glad we'd skipped school

that Friday. Now I could relax and be myself.

***

"Hey, pack that bong of yours, J," demanded Maya.

"Okay, okay, girl."

With lightning speed, Jeremy found his famous two-foot Koi fish bong, while we made ourselves comfortable on his TV room sofa. He unveiled a huge bag of weed from an Asian wooden box on the coffee table. Inside were many smaller bags and prescription bottles of pot.

"Is that Medical Marijuana?" Tom asked, when Jeremy handed him the first toke.

"Yeah, my mom's got chronic pain." Jeremy made quotation signs with his fingers. "We share it. You have to be eighteen or twenty-one to get a prescription yourself."

"Nice of her," Tom said.

"Well, it's legal, right?" Jeremy laughed.

Maya pulled the bong away from Tom as he sucked the smoke from the pipe.

"Chill out, girl!" I exclaimed.

"I really need to crack out today." She lit the bowl again and nearly inhaled the entire pipe. She passed it to Jeremy, while still holding the smoke in her lungs.

"What's wrong?" I asked her.

"My dad lost his job," she blurted out. "And my mom is on a shopping spree as a coping mechanism. And I saw Todd."

"What?" I asked.

"I saw him at school with his new seventh grade girlfriend!"

"He likes them young and fresh-faced," Jeremy said. "Easier to deflower."

"Like me?" She asked. "What's your story?" she questioned Tom. "I still don't know who you are." Jeremy passed the pipe to me.

"He's the new boy, his parents got divorced, and he's from New York. That's all we know," Jeremy explained.

Tom just shrugged and smiled.

"Man of few words. I like that," Jeremy said.

I inhaled the thick smoke deeply. Soon I felt lightheaded and funny. I tried to think of a clever joke, but couldn't quite get the words together in my brain or out of my lips. I held the smoke in too long, and it started hurting my throat. I coughed like I had emphysema. Jeremy passed me a beer out of thin air.

Lost in my random thoughts, I stared at Jeremy and Maya, who were giggling and searching through his iPod. I wanted to tell Tom that I thought he was cute, but the words couldn't form.

"Is this all we're doing, J?" I shouted.

"What do you want to do?"

"I want a snack and then I'll call English Dave."

"Go to the kitchen and find us something then."

"Oh great. I get duped into finding food for everyone."

I stumbled into the kitchen, with Tom following me.

"I'll help," he said.

"Thanks!"

***

I don't know how long we were in the kitchen. I knew we were heating frozen pizzas, because I smelled something burning in the oven. I opened it and smoke billowed out. Tom and I laughed as we took out crispy black pizza.

The music got louder as more smoke of a different kind emanated from the room next door. We were talking and talking. I knew Tom better – though I suppose I was doing most of the talking. I'm not sure about what really. I knew that Tom and his mom were living at his grandparents'. He wasn't sure about L.A. He told me he was seventeen, a year older than me. He was missing New York City terribly and his friends, who sounded kind of boring to me. But I was pretty sure I didn't say that.

I babbled about our dreary school full of dreary kids and about my geeky parents. We realized we were both only children, which must have meant something, psychology-wise. Probably, that we were both brats. He liked the same music as me, and he loved *Wall-E*. I thought that was kind of weird.

We walked back into the other room with the rather burnt pizza. Jeremy had disappeared, and Maya gave me a funny look.

"You've been gone forever!"

Jeremy entered from the back sliding glass door with a plastic grocery bag filled like a balloon. He asked me, "Did you two have sex yet?"

"Funny," I said.

I finally registered the bag and understood what it was.

"Oh J, is this a good idea?"

"What is it?" Tom asked.

"Freon," Jeremy said, making Maya laugh and jump for joy.

"You two are embarrassing," I said.

"You mean CFCs?" Tom asked.

"You don't have to do it," I said. "It's so bad for you."

"Yeah, it's banned, isn't it?"

"There are still a few A/C units around here with it," Jeremy said, inhaling the gas from the bag on the sofa. He exhaled and handed it to Maya. She took her turn and passed it to Tom. He cautiously sniffed a little and gave it to me.

"Whoa. It's really strong," Tom said, turning a little pale.

I pretended to inhale. "This is too *Slumdog Millionaire* for me."

I handed it back to Jeremy, and I felt instantly like my head was going to explode. My stomach turned a bit and then I knew I got a hit. My weed-high was shot. I basically felt like shit.

Jeremy inhaled deeply again.

"Welcome to L.A.," he grinned. He went pale and fell back on the sofa. His eyes rolled up till we could just see the whites. I shook my head.

"This is not good."

Next Jeremy pissed himself, and I thought we might have to call 911. He began making gurgling noises and spit was coming out the side of his mouth. Maya stared blankly at him, dumbstruck. I didn't know if she was even aware what was happening. Thankfully, Tom was another voice of reason.

"Should we call 911?" he asked me, calmly but a little scared.

"I don't know?"

I ran over to Jeremy and shook him.

"Jeremy, Jeremy! Wake up, are you okay?"

He made strange smacking noises, and I yelled at Tom to find the phone in the kitchen. He ran off while Maya was still paralyzed. She started to cry softly. Tom found the cordless phone and I tried to dial with shaky hands.

Suddenly, Jeremy's eyes looked normal again, whatever normal was. He blinked at me and the color came back to his ashen skin.

"Jeremy?"

"What," he whispered.

"Are you okay? Should we call for an ambulance?"

"No, no, I need a drink."

He sat up and saw that he had peed on himself. He was embarrassed by all the attention. Maya jumped on him to give him a big hug, crying loudly now.

"I'm okay, I just had a little accident. I'm always saying I need to try some Depends. Don't cry over spilt urine."

***

I opened the Audi's window to get some fresh air as I drove us back to school. Everyone was quiet in the car. The breeze and the warm sun was refreshing, and I slowly felt human again. I pulled up to the deserted school and only then I realized how much time had passed: it was almost five o'clock. A few cars were still parked in the lots. I stopped in front of Tom's pickup.

He stepped outside the Audi, looking like he'd been through a lot for his first day of school. Maya and Jeremy were asleep in the backseat. Tom walked over to me in the driver seat.

"What are you going to do now?"

"Drive home and try to recover."

"Do you want to hang out this weekend?"

"Oh, sure"

I remembered that he didn't have my email or cell number after he turned towards his truck. I yelled out.

"310…"

He struggled to find a pen from his book bag.

"I forgot, no number, huh?"

He found a scrap of paper, and I began again.

"310-424-2188. Did you even want it?

"Of course, I did. I just…forgot. Brain a little fried."

"Bye," I waved, giving a little smile. I was exhausted now and wanted to get home straightaway.

"Can I text you later?"

"Sure, bye"

He waved to me, looking like he wanted to come back over. I hoped he wouldn't. I just wanted to drive. I did something to the car, which made an awful noise. I blushed. I looked at Tom and he was watching my every move. I waved again and finally took off, with Tweedledee and Tweedledum in the back, snoring now.

3

A tap at my door woke me up. I wiped my mouth and looked at the time. It was eight o'clock! No wonder it was so dark.

"Tierney!" Maya and Jeremy screamed as they barged into my room.

"Your parents let us in as they were leaving for their date night," Maya explained.

"Yuck, they told you?"

"It's so cute," Jeremy said. "They'll stay together forever."

They jumped onto my bed as I was trying to wake up. Jeremy tickled Maya, causing major giggle fits and shaking on my bed. My stomach was turning and I had a horrible taste in my mouth.

"Why are you two fresh as daises? I feel like shit."

"We threw up in your neighbor's hedge," Jeremy admitted.

"I felt so much better afterwards," Maya said.

"Is that why I feel…" I ran to my bathroom. It all came out. I always hated barfing. It was a sign of weakness. I splashed myself with cold water and checked myself in the mirror. My eyes were red and my skin was pallid. My stomach was grumbling. I needed food immediately.

***

In the kitchen, we devoured leftovers my mom had left for me for their date night. Eating my favorite Trader Joe's chocolate ice cream out of the carton, Jeremy grabbed a spoon and joined me.

"So where to tonight, ladies?" he spurted out, with ice cream coming out of his mouth.

"You are so nasty. I thought gay guys were supposed to be neat," I said.

"Not this one, honey. Hey where's Tom?"

"I don't know. Is he your new BFF?"

"I thought he was your new boyfriend," Jeremy said, with an evil grin. Maya laughed.

"We just met the guy, and you picked him up."

"You need to lose it already, girl. What are you waiting for?" Jeremy said.

"J, not everyone is a slut like you are," Maya announced.

"Oh no, you are not the one to talk!"

I checked my iPhone for any texts from Tom. Tracey from New York had sent a hello to me. No word from him, but I saw an alarm from my calendar.

"The Horrors are playing at the El Rey tonight. I completely forgot. Can we still make it? It's nine o'clock!" I yelled at my friends.

"Of course we can. But do you *have* to change?" Jeremy asked.

"Yes!" Maya and I shouted at the same time.

***

We heard an opening band finishing up as we walked into the crowded concert hall. We went to the bar first, sucking on heart lollipops Jeremy gave us in the car. Apparently they were Valentines from his mom's Medical Marijuana co-op last month.

I sucked on the red candy and scanned the room, while Maya and Jeremy tried to catch the bartender's attention. I couldn't believe it. I saw Tom with some blond girl. I grabbed Jeremy's sleeve.

"Hey, is that Tom?"

"Oh yeah, small world. Who's the blond?" He handed me a tall lethal cocktail. "Look Maya, Tom's with another girl."

Maya looked over his way, and said, "You're prettier Tierney."

***

The lights dimmed and the curtains opened with the band walking out. They began with a creepy electronic wall of sound, while blue subtly illuminated the dark stage.

"Let's get closer," Maya said, and I nodded.

Layers of guitar riffs and drumming mixed together. By the time, we reached the stage, Faris, the lead singer, was out pacing, dressed in a thin black suit like the others, underneath the strobe lights. His deep brooding voice broke the beautiful tension.

I couldn't help but be in awe of the band's sound. The lead singer gazed at his loafers, while the rest of band stared at their instruments. They continued into the next song with hardly any acknowledgment of the sea of people swaying and enjoying their music. Our lollipops were kicking in and I hugged Jeremy and Maya, feeling nicely stoned.

A downbeat song, *I Only Think of You*, reverberated through me. Faris brushed his mop-top to the side revealing soulful eyes. He looked to me, stirring a silly teenage excitement within me.

***

Faster beats and louder distortion crescendoed in the El Rey. A mosh pit formed in the front and a girl in a white dress and black boots climbed her way onto the stage. She twirled and danced, grabbing onto Faris, who ignored her and continued singing. Security rushed to stop her free dance, but she escaped with a swan dive. Screams caused Faris to stop singing and the music died. The crowd pushed back and the girl was unconscious on the concrete floor.

The overhead lights turned on, and the band disappeared with the night. Security called for help while another girl cried over the body of her friend. Jeremy dragged Maya and me along with the crowd, who knew it was all over.

"I think it's time to go," he said, with urgency.

I gave a longing look at the abandoned instruments, and we quietly exited.

Outside, the cooler night air was refreshing after the mayhem.

"What is it with today? Is it pass-out Friday?" I asked my friends.

"Do you think she's alive?" Maya asked.

"Tragic," Jeremy said, sincerely.

"I hope she's okay," I said, watching paramedics rush inside.

As we waited like the other fans on the sidewalk, we spotted Tom again.

I waved awkwardly when he smiled my way. Tom and the blond girl I'd seen him with earlier headed towards us with another guy.

"Hi," I said, feeling fuzzy all over. People were clearing out of the concert hall. "That was strange."

"Yeah, I saw them in New York recently, but nobody got injured there," replied Tom. "That I know of. Sorry I never texted you tonight," he went on. "My cousin, Sara, called me with these tickets. It was all last minute. This is Sara," he said, pointing to the blond, "and her boyfriend Philip. They go to CalArts."

"Oh cool," I said, more relieved than I wanted to admit that she was just his cousin. Jeremy and Maya were holding hands and acting nervous. We must have seemed really stoned or insane.

"We need to head back, sorry," Sara said.

"Can I call you later?" Tom asked.

"Hey, we can take you home, if you want to hang with us cool kids," Jeremy grinned.

Tom's cousin looked relieved by the proposition.

"Is that okay with you?" Tom asked.

"Of course, darling, anything for you!" Jeremy said.

We said goodbye to Sara and Philip, and Jeremy and Maya started laughing hysterically.

"What's so funny?" I demanded.

"I don't know," said Maya, nearly crying.

***

"Where are we going?" Tom said, his expression looking almost unbearably serious to me and probably Jeremy and Maya, too. We all stared blankly at each other for guidance.

"I don't know?"

"The Jamaican bar?" Maya asked. "The one on Gower, near Roscoe's Chicken and Waffles."

"Tierney, call English Dave," Jeremy said. "Please!"

"Oh, it's going to be one of those nights," I said.

"Yes, it is," Jeremy said. "Are you in Tom?"

"Sure, why not?" he replied.

We staggered around, trying to find Jeremy's red Audi. We were lost, so he took his remote out and pressed the button till we heard a car beep. It was parked right in front of us.

I asked Jeremy, "Are you okay to drive? Should I drive instead?"

"You? You look wasted," he said.

"Me? You look fucked up!"

Maya laughed at us both.

Jeremy hopped into his driver's seat. It was his car, but our lives were at stake.

"Get us there in one piece," I warned him.

"I know you don't want to die a virgin," Jeremy laughed.

4

Of all the dealers I knew, English Dave was my favorite. His apartment was just off Sunset Boulevard, and he was so popular that his apartment #312 doorbell button was completely faded from all the drug fiends pressing it.

Jeremy and Tom waited in the car, while Maya and I went upstairs. He immediately buzzed us in when I told him it was me.

I knocked at #312, and English Dave opened his door wearing one of his funny German helmets.

"Hello there, do come in," he said, in his proper English accent.

"Hi, how are you?"

Maya followed me in, and English Dave's two guy friends were on the sofa drinking beer and playing video games. A cute blond one, wearing a Kid-Robot T-shirt, asked if we wanted drinks.

Maya quickly said, "Yes, please."

"No, I'm okay, thanks," I replied.

I wasn't planning on being here forever. But Maya was making herself comfortable on a soft chair. English Dave located some Heinekens from his refrigerator. He handed one to Maya and one to me, though I didn't want one. I'm guessing he wanted us to hang out with them.

"Hey, Dave, this is my friend Maya. I hope it was okay to bring her," I said, knowing he liked cute girls at his place.

"No worries, that's Tim," he pointed to the blond one, "and Harry."

"Hi, I'm Tierney."

"She's named after Gene Tierney, the old movie star," English Dave said. "Isn't that glamorous?"

Harry and Tim continued playing Guitar Hero on their Wii. Tim stood up with the electronic guitar, and Maya and Harry cheered him on. English Dave gave me his obligatory polite-drug-deal chitchat.

"So, how is everything?"

"Good, and you?"

"I'm fine! Where's your boyfriend, Jeremy?"

"Waiting in the car, and, you know he's not my boyfriend."

"No?"

I shook my head.

"I have something I want to show you," he said, leading me towards his bedroom.

"Um, okay." I followed cautiously.

He disappeared into the room and returned with a strange military cap. He replaced the helmet on his head with this new hat.

"Like it?"

"Yeah, what is it?"

"German Stormtrooper Captain's cap from World War II."

"Nice."

English Dave set the hard helmet on his mantle next to his other German SS memorabilia. Normally this kind of weirdness was way too Columbine for me, but I knew he was Jewish. So, I guess it was okay.

Maya was enjoying herself with English Dave's friends, smoking weed out of a stainless steel contraption.

Using a professional tone, he asked, "What can I get for you today?"

"Eight hits of ecstasy, please."

"Oh, a real party. You're in luck. I just got really pure stuff in. You'll have a blast!"

"Yeah!"

He handed me eight white pills in a little plastic baggie.

***

Soon, Maya and I were boxing on the Wii, forgetting all about Jeremy and Tom downstairs waiting in the car. I didn't have a chance. I was her punching bag for all her teenage angst.

"Who's next?" she asked the boys confidently.

Tim stood up to take up her challenge. He opened strong, but she killed him.

"The champion!"

"No, no. I'm the reigning champ here," English Dave laughed.

"Bring it on!" She screamed.

"I don't want to beat a girl, but…"

"I can beat you with one arm tied behind my back!"

"Not necessary."

They readied themselves in their best video game boxing stances and waited. The bell rang and they went at it with the controllers.

I was screaming," Go Maya, go!" Their hands and arms were punching the air, pretending to hit each other.

Tim was shouting, "You can do it, Dave!" Meanwhile, Harry was packing another bowl.

Maya launched into a crazy boxing dance, Wii style. She was running in place and her arms were flailing all over the place. Dave imitated her when he saw she was getting ahead. He was so determined to win. I stepped away from them, not wanting to get hit.

Tim was screaming for his mate at the top of his lungs. I was hollering for my girl. Harry was just relaxing and smoking for us all. English Dave had crept slightly ahead. But Maya's madwoman dance was getting faster and wilder. I laughed so hard, and Tim was getting louder and louder. She started with the huge Rocky punches and English Dave was going down, down, down. His cartoon boxer was fading like his apartment buzzer number downstairs. Finally, Maya knocked him out. It was a TKO, and Maya won.

She shrieked with joy.

"I am the champion! World title, baby!"

"There, there, you had to fall one day," Tim patted English Dave on the back.

"Rematch, I declare a rematch!" yelled English Dave, but he was laughing and taking it like a man.

A knock at the door startled our cheering. Dave got to the door quickly.

"Who is it?"

"Tierney's lover!" Jeremy exclaimed, through the still-closed door.

"You know I don't like all your friends up here," Dave whispered, looking straight at me.

"I'm sorry. I told them to stay in the car," I responded. "We've been here forever."

Maya hugged the guys, and I made sure I had my goods.

I said goodbye to a slightly pissed off English Dave. As Dave opened his door to let us out, Tom looked uncomfortable and Jeremy was queening out.

"Bye, Thanks!" Jeremy shouted, causing more dirty looks from Dave.

"Shh," I said. "What's your problem?"

"I was getting bored waiting for you bitches. You were taking so long," he said, as we piled into the elevator.

Tom was playing silent.

"I knocked out Dave on his Wii," Maya laughed.

"You know he doesn't like a million people in his apartment," I told Jeremy.

"Okay, I'm sorry Tierney, for the millionth time. Tom was getting sick of me," he grinned at Tom. I was afraid to ask for details.

***

We gathered all the accoutrements for our ecstasy party. We had plenty of bottled water, of course, and I had my favorite purpley fruit punch Vitamin Water, that I was addicted to. And we had loads of music on Jeremy's iPod.

"Let's take it now," Maya said, over Grizzly Bear blasting in the car.

"Yeah this is a perfect spot. We'll be kicking in full gear when we get to my house," Jeremy said.

We were still on the 101 Freeway, close to our exit. I found my baggie, and I offered it to Tom first. I picked one and then passed it on.

"I'm a virgin," he said.

"What?" I was caught off guard.

"I've never done X before."

"Really? You'll be fine. It's fun. I'll help you out."

"I know."

Maya, J, Tom, and I swallowed our pills together at the same time, feeling instantly excited and giddy. I always got this way when we first took E. The drug hadn't taken effect yet, but it was the anticipation that anything could happen.

5

Tom hugged me with his strong arms as we danced. Maya and Jeremy were fighting over music. Swirls of the song, *The Good Ones* from The Kills were booming away, and Jeremy and Maya were singing like the two band members.

I felt a wave, as a silky blanket seemed to pass over me. The ecstasy was working. I had a smile that I couldn't turn around, and Maya and J pushed their pointer fingers to the sky in recognition of our first rush. We were all waving our fingers around to the beat of the music, amusing Tom.

With his head in his hands, Tom left the room without a word. I was concerned but I couldn't stop feeling so good. Maya noticed Tom's quick exit.

"What happened?"

"I don't know?"

"Come dance with us."

"Okay!"

I grooved with them but then I remembered Tom's absence.

"How long has Tom been gone?" I asked Maya and Jeremy. They shook their heads. Time was so elastic on E.

"Should I check on him?"

"I want to take my clothes off! Where's Tom?" Jeremy asked, as if I hadn't mentioned him only a minute or so ago.

"I don't know."

I was confused, but determined to make sure my future boyfriend was still alive. I had given him the stuff so I was responsible for him. I wanted him to be okay. I didn't want to be the one that gave him a bad trip.

***

Tom was in the hallway bathroom, staring at himself in the mirror. His hair was wet and his eyes looked huge. His expression was unreadable, and this made me worried. I stroked his wet hair, which felt slick and funny.

"Are you okay? I don't want your first time to be bad."

"How long have I been here?"

"I don't know?"

"I felt a little ill but I wet my hair and I feel really good now. Wanna try?"

"Um, okay."

He turned on the warm water in the sink looking rather serious. I dangled my fingers under the tap. I was on a tropical island. I let out a slight moan, and Tom played with my hair.

"It feels so… good."

"Yeah." He gently brushed his lips with my hair like a paintbrush. I giggled. Cupping a free hand with the warm water, he dripped the water onto my hair. I pushed my hair back. Tingles went up and down my spine. He combed my hair with his hands, and unexpectedly we started kissing. Our lips were locked tightly and I wrapped my arms around his warm neck.

I didn't know how we got to this point but we were meant for this moment. Waves of pleasure came over me as I surrendered to him my very being. We were gently rocking on a sailboat or in a lullaby on a tree top… when the bough breaks the cradle will fall…

I stood on my toes to be closer to him and he pushed me into the doorframe of the bathroom. I heard my heartbeat bond perfectly with his, if this was even possible. I absorbed his tender body and his mouth curved deeper into me. I could hardly breathe, we were so entwined. Regrettably, I had to shove him off.

"Sorry, I can't…" I took a huge lungful of air. "I need some water."

"Me too."

He was flushed and we were both panting. I giggled and pulled his arm. I heard the sound of the water again, and I found myself in the mirror with Tom behind me. He hugged me from behind, and we swayed to the music from the other room. I couldn't help gazing at my beautiful reflection until I noticed Tom's image again. He looked so happy and lovely. I smiled up at him and he kissed my neck.

"You taste and smell so wonderful."

"I know, I'm a marshmallow."

"You are so squishy," he replied, squeezing my cheeks. We laughed so hard that we were crying, and we fell on the floor.

Happy shouting from Jeremy and Maya and my favorite song of the moment, *Personal Jesus*, from eighties band Depeche Mode, lured us back to the living room. We crawled like tigers, to find Jeremy and Maya in their underwear with another boy. I wondered if I was hallucinating.

"Who is that?"

"I'm Gabe," he said. "You must be Tierney."

"Hi, when did you get here?"

"I don't know, a while ago?"

Jeremy and Maya shrugged their shoulders in unison. They were all hot and sweating, which was making me thirsty.

"You've been gone forever," Maya said. "What have you two been up to?"

"The nasty!" yelled Jeremy. They laughed hysterically and fell onto the sofa together.

"I'm so hot J! Turn up the A/C!" I shouted above the music.

"Yes, Miss Tierney!"

I drank my refreshing Vitamin Water trying to cool down. I laid back onto Tom's lap, and I watched everyone moving and yapping away, like some sitcom.

"I love water. Do we have lollipops? You look hot. I like that bra. Where did you get those shorts? I'm glad we met you Tom. Who is this? Can we have a different song? The trees in *Twilight* are really tall. I hate my Dad. My Dad lost his job. Working sucks. L.A. kicks New York's ass. I'm dumping my Uggs. Let's go swimming. I slept with Todd last month and I'm pregnant."

"What?" screamed Jeremy. He held onto Maya's wrist. "Did you just say you dumped your Uggs and they made you pregnant. How is that possible?"

"Todd, you dummy! He got me preggers!"

"You are a slut, Maya!"

"I'm not the only whore."

"Who, Tierney? Are you keeping it?"

"No, are you crazy?"

"Yes, but I'm functioning."

"Don't worry, Tierney is going with me to the appointment."

"I am?" I asked.

"Yes. You think J could handle it? And Tracey moved to New York. You are the only other girl now."

Tom and I tuned out the others again, and he leaned down to kiss me. It was so nice and wet and warm. Next thing I knew, we were lying side by side on the sofa giggling.

There was an echo of noise around us as I stared into Tom's face. He touched my chin and I closed my eyes. I saw bright flashing lights like in a disco. The music vibrated in my stomach. Then someone bounced next to me. I opened my eyes slowly, and J, Maya, and Gabe were jumping up and down on the sofa like Tigger from *Winnie-the-Pooh*.

"This is not make-out time!" Jeremy exclaimed.

"Don't fall on me!" They came really close, when I heard it.

"Stop, stop the music!" I shouted. "I hear something."

Jeremy ran and turned everything off. We were concentrating.

"What is it?" Tom asked.

There was a bird singing its pretty song outside the sliding glass doors.

"It's a bird," Gabe said.

"What time is it?" Tom asked. Everyone looked at one another. Jeremy checked his phone, it was five a.m.

"What time does it get light now?" Maya asked. I was sobering up. I was achy and my jaw was sore. Everyone looked like they were feeling the same.

"Hey, I have some more E," I whispered.

"Let's go somewhere first," Jeremy said.

"Where?" said Tom.

"I'm not in a fit state to venture outside," Maya groaned.

"Come on, we can make it," Jeremy replied.

"I only have four left, though," I said, looking at Gabe.

"No worries, I have five of mine. We can all do those," Gabe said.

"Are they good?" I asked.

"The best!"

Everyone popped more pills and started dancing to the pounding music. Tom and I found a bedroom away from the rave. We were quiet, taking in our mellowness. We looked at each other again in our own silent conversation in our own world away from the chaos of our friends. He beamed at me.

"I'm glad I met you."

"Me, too. Did you like it?"

"Yeah, it was amazing," he said.

"I was afraid you were going to be sick."

"I know, but I felt better after I wet my hair and yours and when I kissed you." We kissed again gently. "It was nice in the bathroom."

"Is he your boyfriend now?" yelled Maya, suddenly appearing at the door. "Tierney wanted to know if you liked her."

"I think he really likes her," Gabe said, next to her.

"And I like you," Jeremy said to Gabe. They started kissing in the doorway.

"No, none of that! I'm the odd girl out here," Maya whined.

"No you're not. You have your baby," Jeremy said.

6

I woke up in my bed with a swollen jaw, a stomachache, and wearing Minnie Mouse ears that I had absolutely no recollection of ever seeing before. After the second pill, I didn't remember much of last night.

I couldn't find my cell phone, and I dumped out my entire purse looking for it. I found all sorts of strange things, and my phone was at the bottom covered with something unknown and sticky. I wiped it on my bed sheets and I checked for text messages. I sent a quick text to Maya and Jeremy, asking what they were doing.

***

Unable to face my parents, I hid in my bedroom. I woke up when I heard my phone beeping. A text message from Maya said to call her. It was 6:15, and I heard my parents in the house. Still in a daze, I tried to walk normally into the kitchen. My dad was setting the table, and my mom was busy cooking .

"The sleeper has awoken" Dad said.

"Yeah, ouch!" I said.

"What's wrong?"

"I hurt my jaw yesterday."

"How?" he asked, looking worried. My mom stopped what she was doing to check me out.

"I think it's TMJ again."

"I think it's too much partying, and too little studying," Mom said, putting her hand on my shoulder. "You're not going anywhere tomorrow. Did you take anything for it?"

"Muscle relaxers just make me fall asleep," I said.

"Maybe take some Ibuprofen instead," Dad said, looking in the cabinet. He found the bottle and handed me one.

I took the pill and poured myself a tall glass of water to swallow it with. My parents finished preparing dinner.

"Can you eat?" Mom asked.

"Yeah, I'm hungry," I said. "I'll have to eat slowly."

"Lucky for you, I made bean soup, and we have some soft bread," she said.

"Perfect," I said, sipping slowly from the left side of my mouth.

"How was your concert? What did you and your friends do afterwards that made you come home so late?" asked Dad.

"They were so cool, but a girl got hurt jumping off the stage."

"What?" My mom asked.

"Yeah, some girl got on stage, then fell onto the floor, unconscious. It was scary. Ambulance came and everything."

"I'm not sure these concerts are the best environment for you Tierney. You need different friends," she said.

"I don't need different friends. We just went to Jeremy's house and danced and talked," I said, concealing our extracurricular activities.

"I know Tierney will work hard all day Sunday, right honey?" Dad said.

"Yes I will."

"You should take it easy tonight, too," Mom said.

"I only know that the TV is calling my name," I said.

***

As we were eating our dinner, I heard my cell phone ring in my bedroom. We all looked up when it rang, but I just left it. I was too tired to run to it, and I knew my parents were unhappy with my late night. Then our home phone rang.

My dad, who was closer to the cordless phone, grabbed it and handed it to me.

"I have a feeling it's for you," he said, grinning.

"Hello," I said, expecting it to be Tom.

"Tierney." It was Maya, who was crying hysterically.

"What's wrong?" I asked, getting up from the table. My parents looked at me, knowing something was up.

"I'm at the hospital," she said. "It's Jeremy."

"What? What happened?"

"Jeremy is in the hospital. I called 911."

"What? Why?"

"I found him unconscious. You have to come here. I'm by myself and I'm scared."

"Tell me what happened."

"I thought he was sleeping all day. Around five, I tried to wake him up. He was making weird noises, and I just knew… I knew something was wrong."

"Okay, calm down. I'll come over now," I said and hung up.

My parents were very concerned by my expression.

"What happened, Tierney?" asked my mom.

"Jeremy's in the hospital, in the ER, I guess," I said, stunned. "I have to go right now."

"I'll drive you," she said, standing up.

I tried to get my thoughts and actions together. But I was muddled and my head was reeling.

"I can go by myself," I managed.

"You don't look in a fit state to drive my car," she said.

"You're probably right."

I staggered to my bedroom to change into some jeans and grabbed my purse. I was in a dream-like daze. Everything was happening as if I was watching myself on video. My mom found her keys, and we said goodbye to my dad.

***

I was still light-headed on the silent drive to the hospital. I couldn't even fathom what was happening. My heart was racing and my mind was everywhere. We had taken two hits of ecstasy yesterday, but I barely knew what had happened afterwards. I still had no idea how I got home into bed. We drank lots of water and Vitamin Water, but no alcohol at Jeremy's house. I didn't know what the others did. I was hoping my mom wasn't going to freak out when she found out that any of us did drugs.

When we walked into the emergency room waiting area, I immediately spotted Maya with Jeremy's mom. I always thought she was glamorous. She's tall and thin, with every changing hair color. That day she was a brunette, and she was hugging Maya, who was distraught.

As I approached them, tears welled up in my eyes. I could sense that the news would be dreadful. I hugged Maya, who moaned louder. I couldn't control myself now either. I was crying and crying. When we took a breather, Jeremy's mom filled us in on what the doctors had told them.

"The doctor said that it was a drug overdose. He's aspirated vomit into his lungs, and there is some brain swelling," she said slowly, trying to be calm. But tears soon fell down her cheek.

"He said that they are waiting for a preliminary drug-test. Jeremy – " She faltered at his name. "Jeremy is in intensive care. Tierney, do you want to see him?"

"I can see him?" I asked.

"He's stabilized right now, so you can visit if you would like," she said, each word spoken carefully, as if she might stumble over any one of them.

I didn't want to see him, but I said yes to her. His mother led us into another area across the hall. My mom was walking behind me, in shock, like me. I was scared to death to see him.

As we approached, I saw the shape of his legs underneath a light blue blanket through the window to his room. I swallowed hard as Jeremy's mother opened the door. I couldn't stop my sobbing as I looked at him, eyes closed, lying, connected to a dozen tubes and all kinds of machines near the head of his bed. A heart monitor beeped slowly and mechanically, and a life support machine pumped air steadily.

He no longer looked like the vibrant Jeremy I knew and loved. He was a pale body, a vessel, with medical technology keeping him alive. So many thoughts whirled in my mind, and I held onto Maya for support. I sobbed hard into her hair.

"I called…911 as soon as I could," she whimpered.

"Oh, dear, you did everything…" said Jeremy's mom. She gave us a hug and we cried together.

After a moment, she broke away from us to hold Jeremy's hand. She smiled sadly.

"Jeremy, Tierney is here now to see you," she said to him. "She wants you to get better real soon."

The way she was talking to him unnerved me. Could he still hear us? He didn't answer – I didn't know if he could even hear me. She went on talking to Jeremy in her almost trance-like way.

"I'm going to wait outside. I think she wants to talk to you."

Then, slowly, she turned to me. "I'll be back soon."

She placed his hand back on the bed and quickly walked out of the room. I looked at my mom, who looked very distressed.

"I'll let you talk to your friend," she said, with tears streaming down her face.

***

I waited for them to leave, and Maya held my hand as I took Jeremy's warm hand into mine. It felt so alive, but somehow I knew it was all over. I didn't want to say it out loud, but deep inside my heart I knew that Jeremy was already gone. His spirit had moved on. This thing I was touching wasn't him, and no matter what we did, it would not make any difference.

"Um, Jeremy, it's me, Tierney," I started. I was unsure of what to say.

"Hi, Jeremy," Maya said, smiling.

I looked to Maya for help.

"We want you to get better so we can all go home together," she said.

"Yeah, I miss you, and I know you're going to be alright," I lied.

I started crying again, and Maya held onto me. I couldn't do it anymore. I slowly placed his hand down and sat in the chair next to the bed. Maya took his hand lovingly.

"We all love you so much, and I know you can pull out of this. I just know it," she said.

"What happened after we took the second hit?" I asked her. " I can't for the life of me remember."

"I, um…" She looked at me flustered. "We did stuff. I don't know. Ask me later."

"Well, when did you call 911?"

"We had been sleeping, or I guess I had been sleeping on and off. Then this afternoon he was so dead asleep…"

"Okay."

"I tried to wake him, but he was just out. You know how Jeremy is. He's such a sleeper, I didn't think anything of it. But after a while I started getting worried."

"You should have called me."

"I think I texted you. I don't know. Around five, I heard some noises, but he was still in bed."

"What kind of noises?"

"Gurgling or something." Tears were streaming down her cheek. "I knew something was wrong. I was afraid, but I got it together to call 911 for an ambulance. They came really fast and asked all sorts of questions."

"What did you tell them?"

"They asked what he had taken, if he was on any medication. Did we take any illegal drugs?"

"Did you tell them?"

"I was honest. I wanted him to get better. I said we did two hits of ecstasy and maybe one Xanax. That was it, that I know of."

"You guys took Xanax?"

"I did, to go to sleep. I don't know exactly what J did. I don't know."

"Right, you did everything…" I stammered. "I'm going to call Tom and tell him. Where was he?"

"Tom hung out for a while after Gabe drove you home."

"Gabe drove me home? Why?"

"You complained about your jaw, and your stomach was hurting."

"My jaw still hurts."

"It was after we played Truth or Dare. You don't remember? That's when it was all so crazy. Jeremy was being Jeremy, and he dared Tom to kiss Gabe. We were all laughing, but Tom didn't think it was funny."

"What happened?"

"Gabe stuck his lips out and Tom slapped him away. Gabe and Jeremy were laughing, but I think Gabe was hurt."

"That's weird. I wish I remembered."

"There was other stuff, but I can't think about it right now. My head hurts too bad. Mostly we listened to music and played around for a bit. We were really beat. Then I passed out on the sofa. When I woke up, Tom was gone and Jeremy was sleeping in his room."

I dialed Tom's number and just got voicemail.

"Hi, it's me," I said. "We're at the hospital." I could hardly put words together. "Jeremy OD'd. Call me back."

I sunk my head in my arm. Maya and I said goodbye to Jeremy and we staggered outside. She led me back to the waiting area, where we found Jeremy's dad yelling angrily at his ex-wife.

"You're never at home! You don't know what he's doing!" he shouted.

"What! You haven't seen him in months, not even for his birthday!" she screamed back.

A nurse came and calmed them down. My mom took Maya and me to the cafeteria to give Jeremy's parents some alone time, and to get Maya some dinner. Maya and I sat at a table, still in shock, while my mom bought the food. When she returned, we were still vacantly staring at each other. Maya ate everything she was given, slowly and methodically. When my mom saw that she'd had enough, we discussed what we should do next. We all decided that Maya and I would stay at the hospital, and my mom would go home. She didn't lecture us or mention anything about the reasons why Jeremy was in this situation. She was truly sad and concerned by the events.

She hugged us goodbye in the waiting area where Jeremy's parents were talking with a doctor. It looked like a serious conversation, and Jeremy's mom started weeping softly partway through it. Her ex-husband put his arm around her shoulders to comfort her. Maya and I took a seat on a nearby scratchy sofa.

"Oh, God, what do you think he's saying?" asked Maya, looking at the doctor.

"I don't know?"

My cell phone rang and it was Tom.

"Hello?" I answered, hushed.

"Hey, I just got your message," he said.

"Yeah, it's… awful."

"How are you?"

"I'm okay." I looked at Maya, with her blank expression. "We're okay." I started to cry again.

"I'm going to jump into my truck right now."

"Um, okay see you soon," I said and hung up.

"Tom's coming over right now," I told Maya, who was just quiet now. We sat and waited, watching the physician talk to Jeremy's parents. He finally finished, and we saw Jeremy's parents embracing. Maya and I looked at each other, a part of us not wanting to know what they'd just heard.

Then Jeremy's mother noticed us and came over.

"We just spoke with the ER surgeon," she began. "He said there is a high level of cerebral swelling, and he's in a coma, which maybe is his body's reaction to the overdose to help him recover. But he also has a very high fever that's not responsive to medication."

Tears were welling in her eyes. Maya put her hand on her to comfort her. I was numb.

"I've asked for a neurologist from downtown, who specializes in drug cases, to see Jeremy, but it's going to take some time," she continued. "Also the surgeon said that a preliminary blood test showed slightly elevated levels of sedatives. So it's being ruled as an accidental overdose," she said, crying harder. "Thank you so much, you two, for being here. It means so much to me."

She gave us both a tight hug. "I know he's going to pull out of this."

She returned to Jeremy's dad, who was on his cell phone. Maya and I were drying our faces when Tom arrived. I jumped up to grasp him, and he enveloped me in his arms. We held each other securely.

"How's Jeremy doing?" he asked.

"He has massive brain swelling from the drug overdose."

"That sounds…" He trailed off, frowning.

"Not so good." I looked at him. He nodded.

The doctor said it was sedatives," Maya said.

***

After a night back and forth between the waiting room and Jeremy's room, Jeremy's father's pastor, who had told Jeremy that God hated homosexuals, arrived in the morning to hold a prayer circle. Jeremy's dad asked us to come into Jeremy's room to join the pastor, Jeremy's parents, and other members of his church. I would have done anything to help his parents at that moment, so we agreed. We held hands and put our heads down, encircling Jeremy's bed for an appeal to God. I hoped God was listening.

7

A couple of days later, out of the blur of the air sanitizers, heart beeping machines, and the prayer circles, Tom picked me up for school. He had met my parents at the hospital, and his polite manner and his caring demeanor charmed them. He was going to be the perfect boyfriend.

School was awful without Jeremy. I was scratching at the walls to escape, and Tom, he was my lifesaver. We ate lunch together and he transferred to Mr. Chambers' art class to be with me.

Saturday afternoon, Tom drove me to his house to meet his family before our first real date. He asked me to try to pretend Jeremy was okay so we could focus on us. We arrived at a house straight out of *Snow White and the Seven Dwarfs*. It was so country cozy that there was even a fake wishing well and little bridge in the front yard. Reading my expression, Tom explained the décor.

"My grandparents have lived here since time began, and my mom grew up in this house. My granddad worked for the studios as a set designer, hence the look. My mom despises it."

"I don't mind it. It's cute," I said.

"Kitsch," Tom said.

"A little."

"Wait till you see the miniature Hollywood sign on the hillside."

"What?"

"It's out back."

"Really, that is so cool."

Tom's grandfather was watching the news when we walked in. The interior matched the outside exactly. There was wood furniture with doilies all over the place. Despite the kitschiness, everything was warm and comforting, and his grandfather immediately stood up and gave me a friendly handshake.

"So nice to finally meet you, Tierney," he said. I wondered what Tom had said about me. I think I even blushed.

"Same here. I love your home," I said.

"Thank you. Did Tom mention that I once met the actress Gene Tierney? I was a young man then, just starting out as a handyman at 20th Century Fox. She was a very nice lady."

I looked over to Tom, who looked a little red himself.

"No, he never said anything," I said.

"I think they were filming *Leave her to Heaven*. She was so down to earth and very beautiful."

Tom's grandmother and mother walked into the living room. They looked a lot alike, though his tall mother looked like the big-city woman trapped in this country–style house.

"Hello," they both said.

"Hi, nice to meet you. I heard you have your very own Hollywood sign. Can I see it?" I asked, probably being rude.

"Oh sure, dear," his grandmother said smiling, leading me towards the back of the house, while his mother was quietly assessing me.

***

Just beyond the grassy yard on the hillside stood a three-foot picture-perfect version of the Hollywood sign, as Tom had described.

"Wow! How long has that been there?" I asked.

"Since the seventies," Tom's grandmother said.

"I grew up with it," his mom added.

"It was my husband's idea. It's even been in some magazines," his grandmother continued.

"I've never seen anything like it!" I exclaimed.

"Tierney is taking me to see the real one today," Tom said.

"That sounds nice, but we've been there before," his mom said quietly. I couldn't read her very well, but I knew she didn't like me.

Tom started ushering me out.

"Let's go before it gets too late," he said.

"Bye, nice meeting all of you," I said, before we left.

***

"Did that go okay? Your mom didn't like me much," I said to Tom in the safety of his pickup.

"It's not that. She's not happy about the move back here," he explained.

"What about your grandparents?"

"They're enjoying having us, with reservations. But my mom's really missing New York."

"Why didn't you just stay there?"

"It's complicated," he looked, at me with sad eyes. "I don't know."

"What do you want to do first?" I asked, trying to brighten him up. "Do you want to check out the real Hollywood sign?"

"Yeah, sounds good." He smiled.

***

We drove up Beachwood Canyon and stopped about halfway up the hill. It was afternoon and quite sunny. We took turns taking funny pictures of each other posing with the famous landmark in our hands, which I had perfected when Tracey, Maya, Jeremy and I did it a couple years ago.

Then we drove east on Sunset Boulevard towards downtown. We looked at all the little galleries and cool shops in Chinatown, and we slurped delicious noodle soup at PHO 76. We danced and watched our shimmering reflections in the brushed polished steel of the rooftop garden at the Frank Gehry Music Center.

The sun was low on the horizon as we pulled up to the Griffith Observatory.

"It's smaller than I thought it would be," Tom said.

"Isn't everything?"

"No!" he exclaimed, laughing and making me giggle.

We ran up to the top of the building to stare out at the smoggy view of Los Angeles. We saw the lights of all the downtown skyscrapers, and to the west, the dark and foreboding Pacific Ocean. We were in an old noir movie.

"Wow this is amazing," Tom said.

"Yeah, it is. Jeremy loves this place. He's really a science geek, you know. Do you think it's okay if we don't go to the hospital today?"

"You don't need to go if you don't want to," Tom said. "Everyone knows how much you cared for him."

"It's tiring. It's so hard."

I was shivering slightly from the cool evening air and from thinking about Jeremy in the hospital, and Tom wrapped me up in his black hoodie that he wore the first day of school. I gently held his hand in mine, and we kissed softly. I hugged him close, hoping this feeling would never end.

"It's nice being with you," I said.

"I've never met anyone like you," he said. We both smiled at this gushy Hallmark moment.

***

It was late when we arrived at my house. The lights were off inside, and I invited Tom in.

"Are you sure?" he asked.

"Why not?"

We snuck quietly into the kitchen to raid my mom's secret stash of Trader Joe's chocolate cupcakes. Enjoying the sugar rush, Tom gave me a funny look.

"What?" I asked.

"Stay still," he whispered. He bent over close to my face and gently licked frosting off the side of my mouth with his tongue. My heart pounded, and I felt flushed.

"Not here," I said, softly.

Looking for a sign of my parents, I pulled him into my bedroom. Tom scanned the room, checking out my worldly possessions. I opened up iTunes on my laptop and played *Tonight* from Lykke Li. The soothing music filled the air. He sat on my bed, and I joined him.

"I don't think you can stay too long. My parents would kill me if they find you in here so late…"

Before I finished my sentence, he seized me tenderly and kissed me. His hands brushed through my hair, electrifying my spine. I opened my eyes finding his eyes piercing into me. I moved onto his lap facing him. I took off his hoodie, and our arms were entwined ever so tightly. I wanted to let myself go but soon my brain was telling me to take things easy.

"I'm going to get into trouble," I panted.

"You're probably right, but I can never sleep," he sighed. "It would be so nice just to lay down beside you."

He held me close.

"I'm so in love with you, you know that?" he smiled serenely.

"I think I'm in love with you too."

We embraced a little longer, and finally Tom got up to go. I stood up with him and hugged him, like I never wanted to let go.

"You smell so good," he said, with his face buried in my hair.

"I don't want you to go, but…"

"I understand, another night…"

"I have your hoodie," I said, finding it on my bed.

"Keep it so you can think of me." His eyes searched mine again.

With another long kiss and hug at my front door, he said goodbye. As he drove away, I couldn't stop thinking how lucky I was. I dashed off to my bedroom, remembering he had told me he

loved me.

 I snuggled myself up in his jacket and smelled his balmy

smell. It was so inviting, and it kept me company as I hugged it to

sleep.

8

I awoke from another nightmare about Jeremy. In this one, I was gazing at the starry sky and a shooting star fell over the horizon. I could hear Jeremy's laughter and I was suddenly at the edge of a cliff over the violent ocean. I could only see his back. I tried to catch up to him but he was always out of my reach. I never saw his face.

I texted Tom to see if he was awake, but there was no response. I didn't want to deal with my parents, so I turned on my computer, finding endless messages about Jeremy on Facebook. I noticed Tracey was online, even though it was really early on the East coast.

Chat History

TIERNEY
hello?

TRACEY
hey you, wuz up? its late over there.

TIERNEY
sorry, slow in returning your messages

TRACEY
no worries. maya has been filling me in. I hope u r ok ☺

TRACEY
I MISS YOU GUYS!

TIERNEY
I wish you were here. why did you your parents have to get divorced?

TRACEY
they hated each other remember? I was miserable. are you at the hospital all the time?

TIERNEY
Yes. I'm going after breakfast. it's so hard.

TRACEY
I still can't believe it all. I'm going to visit soon. spring break is coming up and I can see you. hopefully J will be better by then.

TIERNEY
I hope. what are u up to?

TRACEY
was talking to my man

TIERNEY
I have a boyfriend now!

TRACEY
details plz!

TIERNEY
he's super cool, dark hair/brown eyes, he's 17, a junior,
his name is tom, and he's from NY. He likes the same
music as me and he's really helped me deal with everything.

TRACEY
he sounds great! which school did he go to in NY?

TIERNEY
I think he said Columbus catholic HS.

TRACEY
all boys right? all the hot guys go there! I think matt has a
friend who goes there. send me a pic soon.

TRACEY
how is maya? she sounds in a real bad way. she told me
she's living at the hospital.

TIERNEY
I don't know. I've been so wrapped up with tom. did she
tell you she's pregnant?

TRACEY
YES! she told me she's keeping it!

TIERNEY
What? I didn't know! I will ask today. BTW which school do
u go to?

TRACEY
Elisabeth Irwin. its going well. I met some cool kids and of
course matt. when are u coming to visit?

TIERNEY
who knows? summer maybe? I'll tell my parents I want to
look at schools. I'm going to go. GREAT TALKING!   call u
tonight after I talk to maya!

```
TRACEY
ok chica!  luv you!

TIERNEY
BYE!
```

***

Maya and Jeremy's mom, looking like a pair of haggard sisters, were holding vigil in Jeremy's room at the hospital. Their private conversation suddenly hushed, as I, the outsider, walked into their lair. Jeremy's mother stood up when I leaned over Jeremy's strangely red face.

"Hello, Tierney. How are you?" she asked.

"I'm okay."

"Now that you're here, I'm going to the bathroom. I'll be right back," she said.

"Doesn't he look better? He's on his way to recovery now," Maya said, with a bizarre enthusiasm.

At first, Jeremy had become thin and gaunt, but now the
steroids the hospital had prescribed him had made him look
chubby. He was like a science experiment of different medications
and treatments, all leading nowhere.

"Stephanie and I found a faith healer," said Maya. "A
Ba'hai."

"Steph...who? Oh, Jeremy's mom?" I said.

"Yeah, Stephanie and I have gotten so close."

"When was the last time you were home, Maya? You look
awful."

"I don't know. But I went home with Stephanie yesterday for
a nap and some food, I think."

"You need to take care of yourself. I know it's important to
be here for Jeremy, but you need to think of yourself too."

"Tierney, I'm fine."

"And is it true that you decided to keep your baby?"

Maya smiled, and gently placed her hand over her belly.

"What? Why?" I asked.

"How can I take away a life after seeing how precious it is?" She started crying.

Stephanie and Todd came into the room. They rushed to Maya's side like a bad soap opera.

"Look, dear, he's getting better," Stephanie said.

"I know, I know," Maya said. "Todd is going to help with the baby, Tierney. He's been very supportive." Todd gave me a weak smile.

"I think it's beautiful. This young couple and a baby." Stephanie stumbled over the words, tears creeping down her face. "I'm going to help all that I can. I love Maya, like a daughter I never had."

They formed a group hug, and I couldn't deal with it anymore. I ran out to call Tom, who was still sane as far as I knew.

"You have to get here quick," I said to him on my cellphone.

"What's wrong?"

"Everything, they're breaking down in there. Maya's gotten back with Todd, and they're keeping the baby, and…"

"Why don't I pick you up? I was thinking of going surfing, or trying to. It's a beautiful day."

"I don't know. I'm supposed to be here."

"Who says?"

"You know how important J was to me."

"Yes, but he's in a coma. I don't even know if he's going to get better," he said, suddenly making real something I had thought from the start.

"I know, but…"

"How about another forty-five minutes? Then, I'll get you and we can go to the beach. You need this."

"Yeah, maybe you're right. I can't breathe in here."

"Breathe. Do it for me."

"Okay. I'll see you soon. Thanks for being here for me."

"I love you."

***

Maya and Todd found me outside in the hallway. They hugged me and I felt guilty. We had another good cry and headed to the cafeteria for coffee.

"It's so wonderful you and Tom are getting along," Maya said, with a tired smile. She looked like she had found a mirror and freshened herself up. "Todd has been so helpful to me."

"I even found a good OB/GYN for the Maya," he said, sounding ridiculous.

"Oh that's great. But are you sure about the baby, Maya? You're so young. What are you going to do?" I asked.

"I love this child. We did this and now we should be responsible," she said.

"But you're only sixteen."

"I have Todd and Stephanie. I don't think you can understand. It's a life inside of me. I feel him."

"Him? How far along are you?" I asked.

"I'm not sure. But I feel him all the time. I know it's a boy, I can tell."

"Well if you really think you can do this, I'll help out," I said.

"Thank you, Tierney. This is really important to me. I know it's silly, but I already love him."

***

Tom drove us up to Zuma Beach, which was beautiful and misty over the water. We opened the door and stepped out into the calm and peace.

"Tierney?" I heard my name from a familiar voice, but I couldn't place it. I turned around and saw a muscular Mr. Chambers in his wetsuit, carrying his surfboard.

"Hello, good morning," he said, in a very perky voice.

"Oh hello…Mr. Chambers. Going surfing?" I asked, still decompressing from the hospital.

"Yeah, it's such a beautiful morning. You two look like you are enjoying yourselves."

"Yes, we are." I didn't want to deal with seeing anybody, especially teachers. I hoped he could somehow tell, that he didn't just think I was being rude. "See you Monday," I said.

"Tuesday, actually," he replied.

"Not Monday?"

"Teacher work day. I'll be working here." He grinned. "Bye"

"Bye," Tom and I said.

"That's right." I turned to Tom. "I completely forgot there's no school Monday. That's good," I said.

***

On our big beach blanket, we lay on our backs enjoying the soft sand. There were real clouds today, and we watched them float slowly by. I almost heard gentle music in my head and I hummed. I sat up gazing at all the surfers in their wetsuits against the luminous dark-bright water.

"They're like little dancing fishies," I said.

Tom and I watched the ocean and the little people on boards. It just looked magical.

"There's Mr. Chambers" Tom pointed.

We followed him, and he was doing really well on those waves.

"Surfing. This is why you come to L.A., right?" Tom said, preparing his board.

He had brought a board for me too and he immediately got it, like a pro. I had a little more trouble. After a couple of hours, I was able to stand up, just about riding a wave before tumbling into the cold Pacific.

On the sand with Tom, we dreamed of being together for the rest of our lives. We kissed and made sand castles. When the sun started to drop in the sky, we changed our clothes and decided to find our next venue. I suggested the Malibu Pier for some food.

***

At the bar on the pier, I couldn't believe my eyes. I saw Maya and Stephanie, Jeremy's mother.

"What are they doing here?" I asked Tom.

"I don't know, getting a drink?" he said.

Leaving Tom, I practically ran over to them as they were laughing and looking like they were having a fabulous time. I tapped Maya on the shoulder. She turned to me, startled.

"Tierney!" Maya shouted.

"What are you doing here?"

"Getting a drink, join us," Jeremy's mom said.

"I thought you said you were keeping the baby. Should you be drinking?" I asked.

Tom came from behind.

"Hey, you left me," he said to me.

"Hello, Tom, your girlfriend is here. Don't worry," Jeremy's mom said, being really catty.

"I'm not worried," Tom said.

"Do you want to join us?" Maya asked.

"Are you getting food? We're hungry," I said.

"I think we're just drinking right now."

"You're pregnant though," I said.

"I drank when I was pregnant with Jeremy. A little won't hurt," said Jeremy's mom. This made Maya laugh hysterically.

"It seems like you've had more than a little," I said. "There's no room here. Why don't we get a table together?"

"Okay dear, we'll join you." Jeremy's mom gazed at us with a really disturbing expression on her face.

I pulled on Tom's arm away to find a hostess.

"We'll just get a table then. See you in a bit," I said.

We were given a table on the patio with a clear view of the drunken twins, Maya and Stephanie, at the bar. Tom and I silently read our menus and waited for them after I had told them we'd got our table. Everything seemed distorted suddenly: it took an eternity to order from our waitress. I watched Jeremy's mom and Maya having a ball, completely ignoring us.

"Are you going to sulk all through dinner?" Tom asked, breaking our silence.

"No."

But I couldn't help but stare at the two of them. Stephanie put her arms around Maya like a vulture. They clinked their glasses and shouted "cheers" all the time. Jeremy's mom fell off her stool, completely intoxicated.

"Earth to Tierney, hello?" Tom's voice broke my intense focus on them.

"Sorry, " I said. "Don't they know they look like fools? And poor Jeremy is in a coma."

"Aren't you here, too?" he asked. "I don't know. They're your friends."

"You don't have to be like that," I said, irritated.

"Like what?" He acted confused. "Come on, we were having a good time until you saw them."

"They're dissing me."

"You didn't want to drink with them."

"So, they never came to our table."

"Tierney, you're making way too much out of this." Tom stared past me, out at the water.

***

Our food arrived, but I kept watching the bar. Tom was talking to me, but I couldn't hear him. Half way through our meal, Maya came over to our table.

"Tierney, we're going over to Moonshadows. Do you want to join us?" she asked.

"I don't know. We just came from the beach and I'm all sandy," I said.

"It'll be fun. We need it. We haven't hung out in a while, outside the hospital," she said.

"Well, who's inviting us? What did Stephanie say?"

"What do you mean? Why are you acting like that?" she asked, clearly annoyed.

"Is she your new best friend? I thought you were supposed to be the responsible one." I said, angrily.

"What's wrong with you, Tierney? We all need a break from…the whole situation. It's no big deal. Stephanie is nice," she added.

I looked at Tom who shrugged his shoulders. I looked over at Jeremy's mom, who was hitting on a surfer half her age. Then they left together.

"Jeremy's mom is leaving with that young stud," I told Maya.

"Oh that's weird."

She ran off back to find Jeremy's mom. I must have looked pissed off because Tom stared at me.

"Why were you so mean to her?"

"I wasn't mean."

"You make so much of sitting vigil for Jeremy, but then when you take a break like normal human beings, you're all bitchy to each other."

***

We finished our meal without saying another word. Tom paid the bill and we left. In the car, we drove past Moonshadows, where Maya had said they were going.

"Should we go?" I asked.

"Why?"

"Maya said they were going there."

"But she never came back to the table. How do you know for sure?"

"We can just drop in. Stop the car."

"No, I'm tired. Let's just go home. You're just going to start another argument with them."

"What are you talking about? Stop the car now!"

Tom pulled over to the side of the road on Pacific Coast Highway, a little past the club.

"Look, I'm tired of your co-dependent passive-aggressive friends. You're acting like little kids," he shouted.

"Are you yelling at me? Why are you yelling at me?"

"Ever since you saw them, you've been acting like a total bitch. You ruined a perfect day. Who cares if they got drunk at a bar? You completely ignored me all through dinner."

"Why the hell are you saying this to me?" I screamed, tears streaming down my face. "I don't need this from you, too."

"Tierney, you and your friend and your friend's mom had the stupidest, pettiest fight back there. I don't know why you bother."

"I don't know who you are. I'm getting out here," I said, unbuckling my seatbelt.

"No, don't leave. PCH is really dangerous."

"I don't need your help," I said, opening the door to the truck.

"Tierney, don't go!" he roared at me.

"Why?" I was crying now and trying to wipe my tears with his hoodie I was wearing.

"I love you and I don't want you going to them," he said, in a fake soothing voice.

"How can you love someone who is co-dependent and passive-aggressive?"

"It's the way you acted tonight. Come on, you're crying. You don't want to go in there like this."

He was right, I looked a mess now, but I was not happy with his behavior. I knew I should just go home because I didn't really want to see them.

"Just take me home," I said, quietly.

Tom drove back onto the road. We were silent for a while as he drove, and I thought about our first fight.

"I am not happy with those comments you made about me and my friends," I said.

"You don't see it?"

"See what?"

"You guys are all caught up in your partying and your selfishness. I prefer just us alone."

"But I need my friends. I can't be a loner all the time like you," I replied.

Tom didn't say anything, and we drove the rest of the way home with all these questions in my mind about our relationship.

We parked at my driveway, and I gathered all my belongings to leave.

"Tierney, I'm sorry we fought." Tom looked at me imploringly. "I said some stupid things because I was angry."

"Well, I guess I know how you really feel about my friends."

"You weren't exactly nice to them yourself at the restaurant."

"I'm tired." I opened the door to go in.

Tom quickly got out of his truck and stopped me with his long arms. He hugged me so tight I could barely move. I tried to push him off me.

"I can't breathe," I said, muffled inside his grip.

"Sorry," he said, releasing me. "I still love you."

"Okay, bye."

"Bye."

I felt his eyes watching me as I entered my house. I didn't want to turn around. I heard his truck's ignition start and the sound of his tires as he drove out of our driveway.

My parents were in the family room watching a movie. I tried to act happy from my day with Tom.

"Hi, I'm back."

"Hi, Tierney," my mom said, looking up. "Do you want some dinner?"

"No, we just ate at the Malibu Pier. I'm going to take a shower. I'm all sandy from the beach," I said.

"We're watching *Scarface*, if you want to join us. I think you're old enough now," Dad said, jokingly.

"No thanks, I'm going to catch up on some reading for English class."

"Okay, honey, goodnight," he said.

"Goodnight," I said.

"Goodnight Tierney," my mom said.

***

After my calming shower, I found two text messages from Tom. Ignoring them for the time being, I called Maya. She answered her cell phone.

"Hi Maya, it's me," I said in my nice person voice.

"Hey, Tierney, we're at Stephanie's place. Where are you?" she asked.

"I'm at home," I said.

"I'm sorry about earlier. Stephanie was acting a little weird," she said. I heard some inaudible conversation in the background.

"Should we come get you and...?"

"Tom's not here and I'm going to bed soon," I said.

"Too bad. See you at the hospital tomorrow then, okay? I don't like this fighting. It was my fault. You know how I can get, and we're all stressed."

"It's okay, but Tom and I had our first fight because of you two."

"Don't worry, you guys will patch things up. You're so lovey-dovey. Are you okay?" she asked.

"Yeah," I said, with tears streaming down slowly. "I don't know why it bothers me."

"Okay, be good."

"Don't party too hard," I said.

"No, I'm going soon. Bye, goodnight. Everything will be fine." She hung up.

***

As if on cue, Tom called me. I decided to answer it. I took a deep breath.

"Hello."

"Hi, did you get my texts?" he asked sincerely.

"Yeah, I was just taking to Maya and Jeremy's mom, my co-dependent friends."

"Don't be like that. I called to apologize."

"Uh-huh."

"I didn't like seeing you being hurt by them, and I got angry. I didn't really mean it."

"Right."

"You have to admit a little that you guys are a tight bond," he said, "and I came in on the middle of it, and Jeremy's in the hospital. Everyone is just dealing with a lot."

"We'll all be happy soon," I said. "Do you still love me?"

"Of course I do. It was a small fight. I don't want to lose you over this, Tierney. Really, I'm serious."

"I know," I said, unable to hold back my tears.

"I wish I were there to hold you. I really need you right now, with this whole divorce and the move. I'm glad I have someone as special as you," he said, tenderly.

"Yeah, I know. I wish you were here too."

"Can I sneak in?"

"No, my parents are up watching a movie."

"Too bad. You know, you are so right for me. We're good for each other."

"I think so too," I said, wiping my tears away and smiling.

"Let's start over again. Can we do that?" he asked.

"Yes."

"Good."

"I'm tired. It's been a long day. I'm going to bed," I said.

"I'm sorry about tonight. I don't…"

"No, I'm just tired. Everything is fine. I still love you and want us to be together."

"Okay, good night, Tierney. I love you."

"Bye, Tom."

I hung up, not sure how this fight had started or what it was even about any more. It was all going so well. I guess it was going too well. But I thought I had made it right with everyone. Maybe it was just me. I lay on my bed, waiting for sleep to take me.

9

The Ba'hai faith healer was not what I expected. A short well-mannered senior citizen in a moth-ball-smelling suit, he came to the hospital about two and half weeks after Jeremy was brought in by ambulance. Jeremy's parents welcomed him, while the church pastor jealously looked on.

He placed his soft wrinkled hand over Jeremy's heart and said a prayer over and over about God being the remedy. We all waited for the miracle. I had no faith in him until Maya screamed.

"His eyes, his eyes!" she shouted.

Jeremy's mother was crying loudly and there were gasps all around the room. As if on some strange cue, Jeremy's eyes opened and scanned the room for about a minute or two and then shut tight again. The healer was pleased with himself. He passed out his card like a used car salesman and promptly left, feeling his job was done. Everyone was in high spirits.

***

I was enjoying being alone later that afternoon, when Maya and Stephanie called me. They were celebrating at Stephanie's house and asked if I would join them. When I arrived they were drunk, and bottles of wine were all over the dining room table.

"Tierney's here!" exclaimed Stephanie. "Let's bring out the good stuff."

A chilled bottle of Champagne appeared and she uncorked it in a blink of an eye. I sipped slowly watching the mess of these two.

"Didn't I tell you it would work?" Maya asked me.

"Yes I guess it did, but the nurse said that opening eyes in a coma is normal," I replied.

"Don't rain on my sunshine!" she blurted.

"Maya, Tierney, just relax. Jeremy's on the road to recovery now," Stephanie said.

"Yeah, he's getting better. He's gained weight. His stats are normal. His brain swelling is under control, and the specialist is coming next week," Maya said.

"What, you didn't tell me that. When?" I asked.

"We're not sure of his availability yet. But he assured me it would be by the end of next week," Stephanie said.

"I'm going to Carmel with my parents at the weekend. But we'll only be gone a couple days," I said.

"Don't worry, Tierney. We'll be watching and caring for him. Go on your trip. That sounds wonderful," Stephanie reassured me.

"Oh God, my stomach hurts," Maya said, clutching herself. "I think I need to eat something with all this alcohol."

"Honey, I'll whip something up. Just sit tight," Stephanie said.

"Do you want to lie down?" I suggested.

"No, sitting up is better," she said, while Stephanie was making a lot of racket in the kitchen. "You know something? I think I need to go to the bathroom. Can you help me walk?"

"Maya are you okay?" I asked, with concern.

"Yeah, I'll be fine."

I helped her with great difficulty to the hallway bathroom.

"Call me if you need me," I said.

A minute later, Maya screamed loudly: "*Aggh! Aggh!*" I jumped, caught off guard.

"Maya?" I yelled.

I rushed to the bathroom door and tried to open it.

"Open the door, Maya! Stephanie!" I cried.

Maya sobbed loudly, from inside. "No, no, oh God!"

Stephanie ran and opened the door, which was hard at first because Maya's feet were against it. The first thing we noticed was all the blood. Maya was on the floor in front of the bloody toilet, and the bottom half of her body was bloody too. She was crying hysterically into her bloody hands.

"Maya are you okay?" Stephanie shouted.

I realized with a shudder that what was all over the bathroom was what we had foolishly called mini-Todd.

"No, I'm not okay," Maya stammered between her tears and gulps for air.

"I can drive you to the hospital," Stephanie said.

"No, I don't need to go. It's over. It's gone." She fell to the ground crying harder. "It's all my fault. Why did this happen? I'm so stupid. I really wanted him...I *loved* him."

I wanted to go to her but the goriness was making me woozy. I wobbled to the kitchen to look for water.

"Are you okay?" Stephanie shouted to me.

"Yeah. I just need some water. I'll get Maya some too."

Even though it looked horrific, we helped Maya clean herself up. I found paper towels and cleaning supplies, and Stephanie gave Maya some fresh clothes. She was still sobbing but quieter. I sucked in my breath, and I started spraying and wiping the floor.

"I'll clean up and you can shower," I said softly.

"No, I can do it. I'm the mom here," Stephanie said.

"I'll help," I insisted.

***

We gave Maya a long group hug, but Maya didn't want to let go. A little bizarrely, even though I knew she had a prescription, Stephanie suggested some weed to help everyone relax.

"I don't want any more drugs," I said.

Ignoring me, Stephanie lit up Jeremy's koi fish bong, and Maya just sat on the sofa immobilized.

"Give me some of that. I need it," Maya said, as pungent thick smoke started to permeate the room.

"I'm going now. I need to pack," I told them. "Are you going to be okay, Maya?"

"Yeah," she said, without looking at me.

I didn't know which disgusted me more, all that blood or the drugs.

* * *

I asked Tom to meet me at the park near my house. We sat underneath a shady oak tree, near the playground. He gave me a long hug and handed me a CD and a small square box.

"What is this?" I asked, surprised.

"I made it for you. It's all my favorite songs. You can listen and think of me," he said, proudly.

"Thanks, but what is this?" I asked, shaking the unknown box.

"You'll find out when you open it. I hope you like it."

I excitedly unwrapped my gift, which sounded like jewelry of some kind. I was right. It was the most beautiful gold chain with a large gold heart pendant with a "T" engraved on it.

"I love it. 'T' for Tierney."

"Or Tom," he said. "We have compatible names. In the unlikely event we do break up, you can still wear it."

"I hope we don't ever break up."

"I hope not either," he said, holding me. We had a warm, nice kiss.

Tom helped me put the necklace around my neck. The cool metal felt good on my skin. I pulled out my mirror to look. I loved it. Watching me smile widely, Tom kissed my neck from behind.

"It's been intense lately," he said, breaking the sound of the leaves and the children close by. "Do you think Maya will be okay?"

"I don't know, I guess," I said.

"We need a break from all this stuff soon," he said, dreamily.

I laid back taking in the sunny scenery. Tom held my hand, and I turned to him smiling.

"You met the wrong crowd," I said.

"I think I met the right crowd," he kissed my hand, "and the right girl."

"You believe in fate?" I asked.

"Yes. There's nothing random in this world. Everything is meant to be."

His eyes looked deep into my soul, and I wondered what was really in there. He leaned over and kissed my lips, delicately.

***

Maya was M.I.A. from school the rest of the week and she wouldn't return any of my calls or texts or emails. I was so worried I thought about calling her mom, but that would only make things worse. Tom and I drove to her house after school.

I rang the doorbell a few times but there was no answer. We walked around the back and we saw her through the window lying in bed in her all-pink bedroom . Tom tapped on the window.

"Maya, Maya! We can see you!" I shouted. She continued to lie there.

"Is she still alive?" I asked.

"She's faking sleep," Tom said.

As if in a trance, she stood up slowly. She looked sadly at us with her gaunt red face. She had obviously been crying ever since her miscarriage. She pointed to the side of the house, and we walked to the back door to wait for her.

When she opened the door, she smelled like she hadn't showered since that day either.

"What do you want?" she whispered.

"You haven't returned my calls," I said.

"I'm tired and I don't want to see anybody," she said.

"We're going to the hospital. Do you want to ride with us?" I asked.

"I don't know. I guess I should."

"You don't have to. But you should come out. Don't be alone," I said.

"Come on, take a shower and let's go," Tom suggested.

"Okay," she answered, drone-like, as if she had no choice in the matter.

While she was in the shower, I realized how bad the situation was.

"She's still wearing Stephanie's clothes from when I last saw her," I said. "Do you think she'll be okay?"

"She just needs to get out and get some fresh air."

"In Jeremy's hospital room?" I wondered.

***

In Tom's car, Maya acted a little better. We went directly to a coffee shop with a patio, so she could get some sunshine and fresh air. Maya refused food at first, but I enticed her with a doughnut from Blinkie's.

After we ate, she was still depressed and introverted. Tom wanted to hold hands, but I didn't want too many PDAs around her.

"Where's Todd?" I asked.

Maya began crying.

"What's wrong?" I asked.

"He…dumped me when I told him what happened," she cried out. I hugged her.

"What a jerk. You're better off without him."

Maya was still quiet when we arrived at the hospital. The mood was completely changed from my last visit. No smiles, just sad faces. Jeremy had never opened his eyes again or shown any flicker of consciousness or response.

Stephanie looked older and exhausted. She held onto Maya like a rag doll, and we joined our hands again for another prayer circle with the pastor.

10

My Mom was yelling at me to hurry up as I packed my weekend bag for our family vacation. I procrastinated because I didn't really want to go. I wanted to be with Tom every day during Spring Break, but now I had to figure out how many pairs of socks and underwear I would need for the next few dull days.

My parents loved road trips. They loved driving to all the different scenic spots in California, and they always planned on an early start. But I ended up delaying them each time.

They had discovered the Highlands Inn Hotel in Carmel before I was born, and they had returned every couple of years since as some sort of pilgrimage. There wasn't much to do there but watch the cliffs and the birds.

I finally got it all together and ran outside, where they were waiting for me. I put my bag into the trunk and hopped in.

"We're actually off," my dad said.

"You look tired. Did you get any sleep last night?" my mom asked, watching me from the rearview mirror.

"Yes, I got some sleep," I said.

"I heard you on the phone when we went to bed," she continued.

"Yeah, I was talking to Tom," I admitted.

"When did you hang up?" she asked.

"I don't know, not that late," I said, knowing in truth that it was really late. I had probably only got three or four hours' sleep.

"Well, you can have a little rest on the drive up, okay?" she told me, as if I were four years old.

"Okay, Mom," I said.

On cue, she popped in a CD of familiar yoga Sanskrit chanting music, causing me to instantly relax. Sometimes maybe my parents were a little *too* California.

***

I closed my eyes, and soon I was with Tom sitting by the real Hollywood sign. We must have been hiking because we were so close to the huge letters that we could see the ladders behind them that would let you climb all the way to the top. We sat in the shade of the vast "H" and Tom kissed me gently on the lips. We lay back on a fuzzy blanket and took off all our clothes. We were giggling, then suddenly it became unbearably hot.

I looked up at the blue sky and saw Jeremy as the sun. His grin was the dazzling rays and I could hardly look at him. I tried to stare but the light was too intense. He was trying to tell me something, but I couldn't understand. Tom was getting angry with me and ran off naked. I chased after him into the woods, but I couldn't find him.

I ended up at a ranch with Maya, riding horses. We were enjoying ourselves when we met a cowboy, who was Tom. But we didn't know each other. He lassoed our horses, though we shouted at him to stop. Then he tied Maya to a tree, and I ran away through the dark woods. He was chasing me, and suddenly I was really scared that he would catch me. I ran and ran and then I woke up.

***

We were at a gas station rest stop when I woke alone in the parked car. Outside, I saw my dad stretching in a grassy area near the bathroom. I grabbed my purse and walked over to him.

"Awake now?" he asked.

"Yeah, I'm going to the bathroom," I told him in a complete daze. "Wait, where are we?"

"About halfway, a little more than halfway. You had a good nap," he said.

I staggered towards the women's room, where my mom exited as I entered.

"Good afternoon, Tierney," she said.

"Hi, Mom," I said, sleepy.

"You can drive next if you want," she said.

"Okay, let me wake up first," I told her.

"You don't have to. Your father can drive."

"No, no, I want to."

"See you back at the car."

I refreshed myself in the bathroom and splashed cold water on my face to revive myself. Feeling much better, I returned to my parent's car. I heard a text message beep from my cell phone. I checked it in the driver's seat of the Prius. It was Tom, checking in on me. I texted back that we were still on the road.

I adjusted the mirror as my parents buckled up.

"Who was that?" my mom asked, already knowing the answer.

"Tom," I told her.

I started the car and backed out of the parking space.

"Are you keeping in contact with your other friends?" she asked.

"Yes."

"You spend an awful lot of time with this boy," she persisted.

'Well, I like him and he likes me."

I was driving at a good pace on the freeway now and trying to relax, while my mom was giving me the third degree.

"Honey, you're only sixteen. You have the whole world ahead of you," she started.

"Yes, I know," I said.

In the rearview mirror, I saw my dad in the back seat playing with his iPhone.

"He seems a little sad from his parent's breakup," my mom went on. "You should take it slowly. There's something I'm not sure about."

"Well, he's nice to me," I said.

"Yes, but remember you should focus on school to get into a good college, and then a good career," she droned.

"Yes, yes, I understand. Can I just drive?"

"Okay, dear. I love you and want only the best for you," she continued.

"I know, I know," I said.

The traffic was light and the sky was clear this late in the afternoon. I looked towards the coast to gaze at the sun. It was bright, but it wasn't Jeremy. I remembered my weird dream, but I didn't know what it meant. I hoped I had brought enough reading material to get through this weekend.

***

It was dark by the time we pulled up to the hotel. I drove up to the main building so my parents could check in. As I parked, I noticed the amazing moon. It was a mere sliver, but strangely mesmerizing. You could see its full roundness, but the only light was at the bottom, like a skinny smile looking down on us.

Inside the lobby near the restaurant, a man in a dark suit was playing tranquil piano music. There were middle-aged couples and cheerful families all over the warm-toned main building. I looked at an exhibition of black and white photographs of Carmel-by-the-Sea along the wall, while my parents got the directions and keys to our room. Like the others, it was separate from the main hotel, along a series of meandering wood-lined paths through towering trees and fern-like Northern California vegetation.

Our room was just as I remembered from our last visits: architectural faucets like waterfalls, lots of wood paneling, and a hybrid of Asian and Frank Lloyd Wright furniture. There was also a wood burning fireplace and a large hot tub in the palatial bathroom.

My dad brought our luggage in, while my mom and I freshened up for dinner. We were all tired and hungry as we walked over to the casual-dining restaurant. It was really chilly outside but my parents wanted to sit on the patio near some outdoor heaters. The moon was quite high now, and my parents were holding hands as our hostess seated us.

They looked happy and relaxed, and I didn't feel too embarrassed being their daughter. The fresh air smelled clean and invigorating. I scanned the patio, and there were lots of families. My parents were having some conversation about wine when a little girl in white walked up to me holding out her doll.

"Look honey, she likes you," my mom said.

I smiled at the little girl, and then a teenaged boy about my age, maybe a couple of years older, came to our table to retrieve her. He looked like the little girl, but his hair was longer and he had clear reflective eyes like the sky.

"Sorry about that," he said smiling to me. "She's very friendly."

"Oh, it's okay," I said, shyly.

"You two look so much alike," my mom told him.

"Yeah, that's what everyone says," he said politely.

"What is the age difference between you both?" my mom persisted.

"Fifteen years," he said, then he looked at me, with what I swear must have been a twinkle in his eyes. "She's my parents' love child."

This caused my parents and him to laugh.

"Bye, have a good dinner. Come along, Sofia," he said.

"Bye," we all said.

"He seemed like a very nice young man, so mature," my mom said.

"Great older brother," my dad said.

"Yeah," I said.

***

The next morning, feeling recharged from lots of sleep and the extra oxygen from the pollution-free air, we had breakfast on our balcony overlooking the ocean. It was colder here than home, and I wrapped up in my thick wooly sweater I called my sheep.

My parents were having a second honeymoon, and I was their extra accessory. I wished I had stayed at home with Tom, but I admitted it was cute that they still loved each other. They chatted and ate their breakfast with an intimacy I hoped I would have one day with someone special. However, I felt a little left out. My parents were practically eating their croissants out of each other's hands. They were laughing and having such a great time.

I tried to text Tom again but had no luck. There was no service last night, and today it didn't seem to work either. I supposed I would just read.

My parents finished their breakfast.

"Tierney, we're going hiking, let's get ready," Mom said, too energetically.

"Oh, Mom, I'm just going to stay here and read. Is that okay?" I asked.

"Are you sure, it's a gorgeous day," Dad said.

"I'm enjoying the view and I want to catch up on some reading," I said.

"Okay, we'll be back in a couple of hours, we're just going on a trail from the hotel," Mom said.

"Okay, bye," I said.

They looked happy to have some alone time. They departed from the balcony hand in hand, into the room and out the door, while I settled into my chair with my book.

Out beyond the cliffs was the forceful ocean. The strong waves broke back and forth on the dark rocks below, sending sprays of pungent smells. I was drawn to the railing to gaze at the view. I stood up and looked out, taking a deep breath of the assorted scents.

A seagull squawked in the distance, while its more adventurous rival landed near our breakfast tray. I made a grab for a chocolate croissant and a coffee cup before it did. I threw it some leftover bagel, which it gladly devoured.

I poured myself some coffee and ate my croissant with my new friend. I threw more leftovers, and soon another seagull arrived. The two birds argued over territory, but they both remained with me. I said hello to them both and offered more treats.

"Hey, you aren't supposed to feed them," said a stranger, causing me to jump in surprise. I looked up and it was the older brother from last night's dinner on the next balcony.

"You made me jump," I said, throwing another scrap.

"Sorry about that," he said.

"That's okay. I don't care. I'm enjoying feeding them."

"They look like they really like you."

"Yeah, I'm their new best friend. Here you go, last piece," I said, throwing the last morsel of food over the railing. The two seagulls dove off the balcony to catch it in midair.

"You were at the restaurant last night," I said, trying to be friendly.

"Yeah, I rescued you from my baby sister," he said.

"Yeah," I said, hearing a beeping from my cell phone in my pocket. I took it out, and it was showing low battery.

"That's strange, my cell is showing I have no battery but I just charged it overnight," I said.

"That happens here. Since there's no coverage, it sucks the life out. The phone uses more power trying to find a signal."

"I've been trying to text…someone, but I can't get through," I admitted.

"There are some patches of coverage in the lobby because it's near the main road. Try there," he said, smiling.

"Okay, thanks."

"I'm walking over there. I'm going to check my messages. Want to come?"

"Um, okay," I said quickly, not sure what this meant.

"I'll meet you out front," he said, walking into his room.

"Okay, I'll just grab my shoes."

***

I stepped into our room, and peeked at myself in the mirror. He had already seen me in my pajamas, so I guess it was okay. But I decided to put some lip-gloss on quickly before leaving.

I saw him on the wood-lined path in front of the building waiting for me, and I walked over to him.

"Hi."

"Hi," he said. "I'm Jack, by the way." He stuck out his hand and I shook it.

"I'm Tierney," I said.

"What was that again?"

"Tierney. I was named after Gene Tierney."

"Tierney, I like that," he said, nodding.

"Thanks."

"I know where the spots are, don't worry," he said. He led me along the path that took us to the rear of the main building. We walked past a small gift shop and the restaurant we ate in last night. In the main reception area, he took out his phone and walked around as if it were a metal detector checking different points. He stopped and signaled for me to come closer.

He showed me his phone.

"Look two bars, right here," he said. I looked at my phone and I had one bar. I tried to send my text, and I waited. Jack tried his voicemail. He was listening to something using a lot of concentration. My phone beeped, saying my text had failed. My one bar disappeared too.

"No coverage here," I said. Jack just nodded and I walked around imitating him, trying to find coverage locations. I didn't have much luck. I heard him laughing loudly. I was desperate. My phone didn't work anywhere. Jack ran up behind me.

"Tierney, any luck?" he asked.

"No, I can't find anything," I said.

"Try outside in front of the building. It has to work there," he said.

"Okay I'll try. But I think I should just give up."

We walked outside to the front where the cars pulled up for people to enter the lobby. I looked at my phone, and magically, I had two bars of reception.

"Yes!" I shouted. "Hopefully this will work." I pressed the send button and waited. It went through. I checked my voicemail and I had one message from Tom, asking me how my trip was going.

Jack was standing nearby waiting for me, so I decided I would call Tom later from this spot. I put my phone away and strolled back to him.

"It worked, thanks for your help."

"No problem," he said, as we started walking back to our rooms.

"I heard you laugh back inside, what was so funny?"

"Oh, that was just my roommate, telling me about his weekend. It was dumb," he said smiling.

"Why?" I asked. He stopped in his tracks.

"Well, he decided to stay on campus for Spring Break. We go to Berkeley, and he had a date with this girl. But he fell asleep and missed the whole thing. This was a girl he's been chasing since the beginning of the year."

"Oh, that's funny," I said, smiling.

"See, it wasn't that exciting."

"No, it's something I would have done."

We passed a sign for the beach. Jack pointed to it.

"Hey, let's go down to the beach," he said, already walking that direction.

"Um, I'm still in my pajamas."

"The seagulls won't mind. They already like you."

"That's right, I'm their new best friend. Wait, I don't have any more food."

"They'll survive," Jack said.

***

The beach was warmer than the wooden path, and I took off my sheep sweater. It was mostly dark rocks rather than sand here, and the crashing surf was like thunder, it was so loud. Jack hiked around the big boulders looking at all the tiny sea creatures. I tried not to fall over the slimy surfaces.

"Look at that sea cucumber!" he shouted. "I've never seen one in California before."

I looked at the plump orange animal. "Oh, wow, I've never seen one anywhere."

"They eat those in Asia," he said, looking more intensely at the water.

"Are you a marine biology major?"

"No, I'm an astronomy major."

"The stars?"

"Yeah, I love it, the night sky. Ever since I was a kid, I loved finding all the constellations," he said. "My dad bought me a real telescope when I was ten."

"I'm horrible at finding anything. But I did see that amazing moon last night as we drove up here."

"That was actually the first night after a New Moon, with a sliver of light peeking out," he told me. "It's called a crescent moon. It's unusual to see it so early in the moon's phase. It was beautiful."

"Astronomy major sounds fun," I said, smiling brightly.

"It is, except there's a lot of work involved. I'm only a freshman, but I really needed this vacation, even if it's with my family."

"Yeah, I wanted to stay home but I'm so glad I came," I said.

"Hey, I'll show you some constellations tonight. This place is perfect. There's hardly any light pollution, and I think it's supposed to be clear."

"Okay, that sounds great," I said, excited.

"After dinner, around nine-ish. I can call out to you from the balcony," he laughed.

"I hope you were joking. Yeah, that sounds perfect. I'll meet you in front of our rooms."

"Sounds like a plan!"

***

At dinner in the fancy dining room, I tried telling my parents about Jack and our day. They were so blissed out in their own happiness, they barely comprehended what I was saying to them.

"We had a lovely couples massage today after our hike," my mom said. "It was so nice."

"We missed you, though," my dad added.

"I was hanging out with Jack. He helped me use my cell phone," I said.

"Who's Jack?" Dad asked.

"I told you, the older brother from last night. I met him and we walked on the beach looking at the tide pools."

"What about Tom?" he asked.

"What about him?" I said.

"He's not going to be jealous?" My dad smiled.

"We were just hanging out. Anyway, Tom doesn't own me. Tonight, Jack is going to show me some constellations after dinner. He's an astronomy major at Berkeley."

"College man," my mom said.

"There's nothing going on. He's really nice."

"Sounds like lots of fun, Tierney," she said, taking my dad's hand into hers.

I hoped there would be no public displays of affection from them with me around. It was good I had plans after dinner because I was sure my parents wanted their alone time again. I really was the third wheel here.

***

Jack took me to a small outdoor pool that I never knew existed at the hotel. It was always so cold here I was positive nobody ever used it. We lay on a couple of deck chairs to get the full planetarium experience, staring up at the real starry sky.

"Where's Orion?" I asked, trying to sound somewhat knowledgeable.

"You can't really see that at this time of year, too close to the horizon. Orion is really a wintertime landmark," he told me.

"Oh."

"There's the Big Dipper," he pointed up.

"Yeah, that one with the bright star that points north?"

"That's the Little Dipper. Polaris or the North Star is at the end of its handle."

"There's more than one?" I giggled. "So where's the Big Dipper?"

"It's just above the little one, upside down. It's part of the Great Bear," Jack said.

"I don't see a bear, but I've found the Big Dipper," I replied.

"The bear looks like a polar bear with its nose sticking out to the right, standing on his paws. The nose is a really bright star."

"Okay, I think I see it. This isn't easy."

"Yeah, I don't have any paper on me to draw it out."

"It's great you know so much. Where is Libra, that's my star sign?" I asked.

"The signs are usually hard to see because they're so faint, but let me look…" He turned around to look behind us. "I see… there's Virgo, the Virgin."

"Where?"

"Directly south," he said, pointing. "There's the head and the body lying down wearing a skirt, with an arm up, and two legs down. That really bright star is at the bottom of the hip."

"I don't see it."

He took my hand directing my eye line to the right position.

"It's right above a box-like constellation called the Crow," he said. "Wait, there's the Scales too. It's just to the left of the Virgin's legs. It's a triangle on top with two dangly sticks, just above those tall tress."

"I see it," I said, very happy to find something. "Wow, so many constellations."

"Yeah, it's like a big picture book in the sky. I can watch forever."

"Have you…?" I asked. "Do you believe in other life out there?"

"There has to be. I don't know if there are any little green men, but there has to more than just us. We can't be the only lucky accident in the universe."

"It's so big, the Universe," I said.

"Bigger that you can even fathom," he said looking at me now. "I have to tell you something."

I turned to him, unsure of what he was going to say. There was a strange intimacy between us now, almost a tension.

"I once saw a U.F.O."

"What?" I asked, perhaps sounding a little too shocked.

"I'm not some freak, and I never really gave people much cred for anyone saying they saw a flying saucer..." he started.

"What did you see?" I said, sitting up to hear his story.

"A few years ago, I was in our backyard, in the pool, relaxing after a few laps, and I saw something bright and silver in the northeast sky."

"What was it?"

"I didn't know. But I knew it was something unusual. It was hovering in the same spot like a deflated metallic balloon, but it was too static."

"Wow," I said loudly.

"I ran inside to get my binoculars and video camera," Jack told me.

I looked at him intensely, with his gripping story. He sat up, too, getting into his own tale.

"Through the binoculars, it looked like large spinning spheres in a triangular shape. It was mesmerizing and like nothing I had ever seen before. I tried to use my video camera, but it was harder to make out in the viewfinder," he said.

"You have video? Can I see it?" I asked.

"I can email it to you," he said.

"Oh, that would be so cool."

"I'm not a U.F.O. fanatic, but it was pretty spectacular."

"Do you think that's why you're studying astronomy?"

"Yeah, though I was already really interested. But finding more about what I saw would be amazing. I tried to find out if anyone else saw what I saw that day. It was a nice Saturday afternoon," he said.

"You looked on the Internet?" I asked.

"I found one couple who posted something, who lived on the other side of town. But their craft looked different. Maybe it was a different angle. I don't know…"

"A large part of NASA's work is to find life out there, isn't it?" I asked. "There must be something."

"What's your email? I'll put it into my cell phone before I forget." He took out his phone and punched some buttons. "What is it?"

"It's *tierney@charong.com*," I said. "I can't wait to see your video."

Jack typed in my information. "Cool. You know, I better get going. It's late."

"What time is it?"

"It's 11:30. We're leaving early tomorrow morning, and I have to pack."

"I should go too. I don't know what my parents have in store for us tomorrow."

We got up and I looked again at the bright sky. It was so vast and intriguing. We walked silently back to our rooms, and I thought about Jeremy. By the time we arrived at our room, I was crying.

"That was fun... Why are you crying? I know I can be boring, but...," he said quietly.

"Oh, it's just my friend is in a coma right now, back home. Looking at the beautiful stars made me think of him."

"I hope he gets better," he said, sincerely.

"I don't think he will."

"Really? That sucks."

"Yeah it does. But," I smiled. "He'll never be forgotten. I'll always love him. Thanks for showing me the heavenly bodies."

"I'll email you the video when I get back."

"Don't forget. I'm really interested to see it. I've never seen an U.F.O. before," I whispered.

"But don't remember me as the crazy U.F.O. guy," he said, laughing.

"I won't, I promise."

"If you ever want to check out Berkeley, I'll show you around," Jack said.

"Okay, sounds good."

He gave me a big bear hug. "Don't worry about your friend. Dying is natural, and time…time is infinite."

"I know," I said, letting the tears fall down my face. "Sorry for all this wetness."

"No, I like a good wet shoulder. You must be a great friend."

"I should go. Great meeting you, bye."

With a wave, he went into his hotel room.

***

Today was our last full day here, and my parents and I decided to drive into town. We strolled through the cute little streets lined with fancy knick-knack gift shops and wine tasting rooms.

My parents were still in their second honeymoon state of mind, and I walked two steps behind them. We had lunch at a nice restaurant with a bougainvillea-covered patio. My parents gave me a big glass of red wine with my brick-oven pizza. Feeling cozier with my wine, we headed to a beach to look for seashells. We sat on a big log on the sand and watched the sunset.

"Our trip was so perfect," Mom said.

"It was," said Dad. "Did you have a good time with your middle-aged parents, Tierney?"

"I had fun with you two," I said, smiling.

"Are you going to keep in touch with Jack?" Mom asked. "He seemed very nice."

"Maybe. He said he was going to email me, and he said I could visit him at Berkeley."

"That sounds sweet," she said.

**

We actually made an early start for once, and I said goodbye to the hotel with its majestic trees and views. We drove along Pacific Coast Highway through Big Sur, which was so awe-inspiring. The dark clouds and mist gave everything a mysterious look. I watched the sky where it met the coastline.

We dropped down past San Simeon, and my mom let me drive again. I felt more relaxed and centered, and I realized I'd never called Tom back. It was funny that I forgot because I was having such a good time with my family.

By a small beach along Highway 1, I noticed large animals on the sand and a crowd of people gathered in a tiny parking lot.

"What's that?" I asked, pointing.

"I'm not sure. Let's park and find out," Dad said.

We found a spot along the road. It was a lot warmer here than Carmel. The glare made it hard to see at first. There were lots of people along the beach, and a park ranger was talking to some of them.

We stopped by a parking sign. The animals were elephant seals, coming back to mate. They were huge, and their smell was overpoweringly fishy and oceanic. We watched them bask in the sunshine all over the beach.

My parents snapped pictures of the scene. Soon, what I assumed was a male elephant seal started a fight with another male for territory. The larger one – the instigator – stood tall and pushed the smaller one. There was not much of a fight and the smaller one backed off quickly, flinging himself back into the sea with a loud splash. The aggressor made a loud trumpet-like wail, triumphantly. It was a nature documentary right before us. I took a photo of the winning seal on my cell phone and sent it to Tom, with a big "miss you" message. For a moment, I thought about sending it to Jack too, but I didn't.

The remaining drive home was pretty mundane. When we arrived, my parents were asleep behind me. I parked the car in our driveway. I turned around, and my mom had her head resting on my dad's shoulder, like two teenagers. They could have been Jeremy and Maya, passed out after some fun night out somewhere. I didn't want to wake them up.

I stepped out of the car and called Tom on my cell phone. I got his voicemail.

"Hi, Tom, I'm back home now. How was your weekend? Call me later or I'll call you tomorrow. Bye. I missed you so much. Bye."

I put my phone away and opened the trunk to get my luggage. My parents were still asleep. I opened the back door.

"Hello, you two, we're home!" I exclaimed. "Wake up!"

My mom stirred and gently rubbed her eyes and stretched her arms like a small animal. My dad started to snore, he was so content.

"What, we're here already?" she asked softly.

"Yeah, I got us back nice and safe," I said, leaning on the car door.

"I had a nice nap."

"You sure did. I'm going inside, Mom," I said.

"Okay, I'll get your father up," she said.

I turned to go inside.

"Tierney," my mom called.

"Yes," I said, turning my head.

"Thanks for driving us. You're so grown up now," she said.

"Your welcome, Mom. I had fun this trip." She stepped out of the car.

"I had a good time, too. Remember what I said, Tierney."

"Which part?" I asked.

"The part where I said you have your whole life ahead of you, and don't grow up too fast."

"Oh, yeah. I understand. Don't worry,"

"I'm not. I know you're a smart girl and you always know what you want. And I'm also sorry about Jeremy," she said.

"I know."

"Get some rest and don't talk to Tom all night."

"I'm going to bed," I said.

"Good night."

"Good night, Mom."

11

The specialist Jeremy's mother had contacted finally arrived Friday, the end of our Spring Break. Nervous excitement filled Jeremy's room. Everyone thought this man would save him somehow, but Jeremy's father still believed that his God would bring about a miracle.

We all stayed in Jeremy's room waiting while the new doctor did more tests, and more machines were brought in. After a long period of silence and analysis of various printouts and computer readings, there was a whispered conference between two different neurologists. I pulled Maya and Tom aside.

"Do you think we should wait outside and give his parents privacy?" I asked.

"No, I want to be here," Maya said.

"It's up to you. Do you want to leave?" Tom asked me.

"I'll ask his parents," I whispered. I turned to his mother.

"Should we stay or…?"

"Oh, dear, you are welcome to stay," Stephanie said, with an air of desperation.

Her tone made me nervous. I knew it was going to be unpleasant soon. I didn't want to see what was going to happen. The specialists had been working on Jeremy for what seemed like hours. I had butterflies in my stomach, and I sensed everyone else felt the same. After an eternity, the doctors turned to Jeremy's parents. The main neurologist coldly pronounced Jeremy officially brain dead and said that they were going to shut off the life support machines.

Jeremy's parents clutched each other tearfully. Maya was screaming.

"No, no! Is there another test?" she yelled. She was not taking the news without a fight. She started shouting at the doctor.

"I saw his eyes looking at me the other day, blinking in response. He's not dead. He can't be," she said angrily.

"I'm sorry, but the tests all came out negative for any brain activity," the doctor said.

"Please, give him more time. I know he's alive. He opened his eyes. You can't do this. Stephanie, Jeremy is going to be fine. Please don't do this," she begged.

"Maya," Stephanie said quietly, through her own tears.

I was watching a terrible movie scene. Uncontrollable weeping and wailing, while the hospital attendants were preparing to unhook all the life support systems. I held onto Tom, who was calm, like I tried to be. I actually felt better with the certainty of Jeremy's situation, and I pulled Maya to us to comfort her.

"You must get a hold of yourself, Maya," I said to her. "This isn't good for you. Jeremy wouldn't want it this way."

"What's wrong with you? He's not dead," she screamed.

"Stop it, just relax," I said, gently but firmly.

"No, we need to call the faith healer again. That doctor is going to kill him. I know his spirit is still with us," she insisted.

I gave her a stern look, and she seized me, almost violently at first. But then she buried her head in my shoulder and cried. We wept together as we heard the drone of Jeremy's flatlined heart on the electrocardiogram. I whispered goodbye to perhaps my dearest

friend.

***

I stayed home from school Monday. I didn't want to see

anyone or talk to anyone, including Tom.

I lay in bed, uneasy. I tried to watch TV, but I couldn't. I had

no desire for food or water. I didn't know what to do with myself.

I was tempted to call Maya, but since the hospital, she was

even more attached to Jeremy's mother's hip. It was like she was

her new daughter. I supposed they were turning to each other for

support, but I didn't want to talk endlessly about how the doctors

were wrong.

Somehow the day passed, and I got a knock at the door and

it was Tom. Reluctantly, I let him in.

"You didn't go to school?" I said, closing the door.

"No, I went. It's after school, already," he replied.

"Oh," I said.

He embraced me gently, and I just stood there emotionless. I felt like I had no more feelings left. He looked at me with a puzzled face.

"You didn't miss much at school. It was all the same," he said, sitting on the sofa.

"All the same," I said.

"Yeah, but they did mention Jeremy in Home Room over the loudspeakers."

"What did they say?"

"That he passed, and we had a moment of silence for him."

"Oh, really," I said, annoyed.

"What's wrong with that? He was your friend," Tom said, surprised by my reaction.

"What do you mean? Jeremy wouldn't have wanted that …"

"It's just to reflect…"

"Okay, Mr. Sentimental," I said, walking to the kitchen.

"You're just in your grieving phase," he said seriously to me.

"What? No, I just don't care what a bunch of losers who don't even know him or…"

I was crying again, and I realized that I didn't want to see Tom right now. He put his arm around me, but I pushed him away. He got up and walked to the door.

"I'll see you later. Are you going to school tomorrow?" he asked.

"I don't know. Probably not." I wiped tears from my face.

"Can I come over tomorrow?"

"Um, maybe give it another day? I don't want to see anyone." I couldn't tell if he was annoyed or sympathetic, and right now I really didn't care.

"Okay. I understand, bye," he said leaving.

***

I returned to school Wednesday because my parents wanted me to have some normalcy to my routine. My mom stopped the car to drop me off, and I expected to see Jeremy driving up in his bright red Audi station wagon.

"We've decided to skip your father's business trip this weekend to be with you," my mom said casually.

"Why?" I asked.

"I think you need some support right now, and Jeremy's funeral is Saturday."

"Oh yeah, that. It's fine. I would rather be alone."

"I'm not sure that's a good idea," she continued.

"I'm not going to kill myself in a depression, I'll be okay," I replied.

"I know that. But it's nicer to have your family here. We were planning on being gone for five days. That's long."

"I'll have Maya or Tracey stay over," I suggested, though I was lying.

"Maybe. Have a good day at school," she said and kissed me.

***

Out of habit, I looked for Jeremy in first period. Everyone was talking and laughing like normal. A few people came up to me and told me how sorry they were. A girl sat next to me in English and talked to me endlessly about what a wonderful person Jeremy was. I tuned everything she said out.

Our second period meanie, Mrs. Lewis, was extra nice to me. She asked how I was feeling and told me that if I needed someone to talk to, she could lend her ear. I gave her the cold shoulder.

I ran into Maya with Todd at lunch, looking very much a couple, and completely off their heads.

"Hi Tierney, guess what?" she asked.

"Hi Maya, what?" I responded.

"We're back together again," she said.

Todd put his arm around her giving her a big squeeze.

"Oh good," I said.

Maya gave her guy a huge pearly smile, and they started kissing. I was a little grossed out, and I recalled what it was like last year eating with them. Jeremy and I had to have lunch by ourselves, they were so embarrassing. I knew Tom and I were nowhere near that bad with PDAs.

Tom found us and had the same reaction as I did toward Todd being with us. In the lunch line, I cornered Maya alone for a quick chat.

"He's just being nice," she said, slurring her words.

"What are you on? You shouldn't be at school like this," I said.

"Look," she said. "I'm just trying to cope."

"What have you been doing?" I asked.

"I've been with Stephanie," she began.

"Do you think it's such a good idea to spend so much time with Jeremy's mom?"

"I've been helping with the funeral arrangements," Maya said, softly.

"Oh."

"She wants us to say something."

"Together?"

"If you want, what do you want to do?" she asked.

"Let me try to come up with something, but can we do it together? I really don't want to do it alone."

"That sounds good," she said, with a small smile.

I ate in silence, while the others were having a conversation they obviously thought was serious.

"Sid Vicious was just some junkie, not a real musician," Tom said.

"The Sex Pistols were real punk. They didn't care about anything," Todd argued.

"What are you moaning, oops, I mean talking about?" Maya asked.

"Who was better, The Clash or the Sex Pistols?" Tom said.

"That was eons ago," I said.

"The Sex Pistols weren't just a band, they were an idea," Todd said.

"The Clash had real songs…," Tom went on.

While Maya and I just nodded, following this argument, I told her how I felt.

"He's boring," I said into her ear. "I never liked him. Maya, you can do much better."

"I don't care. Tom's not perfect either," she said.

"But you don't need him, really."

"Yeah, well it's not up to you," she said.

"Tom wins," Maya shouted for all to hear. "*London Calling* is one of the coolest songs of all time. You win!" She stuck out her hand for him to shake.

Tom looked puzzled but shook her hand and said, "Thank you, Maya."

Todd went back to giving his full attention to Maya, and they started making out again.

***

As we left the cafeteria after lunch, Tom took me aside and whispered to me.

"Todd showed me the stash of pills he and Maya were on," he said.

"What?" I asked.

"Yeah, he showed me in the cafeteria."

"Why?"

"He was really out of it. I don't know."

"That's weird. He's so wrong for her. I wish she would realize that."

***

Tom and I walked into class really late. I hoped Mr. Chambers would be cool. As we entered the room, he was lecturing about some Art History stuff. He was a little annoyed while Tom and I found seats in the back of the room. As we walked towards two empty seats, I knocked over a stool. The loud crash caused everyone to turn and look at us.

"Oops!" I said.

"Thank you for gracing us with your presence today, Tom and Tierney," Mr. Chambers said.

"Sorry," Tom and I said together.

We sat down, and I attempted to find my notebook and pen. I found a pen in my bag but I couldn't find my notebook. I scrambled forever, creating more unwanted noise. Tom handed me some loose paper and I quickly started writing whatever Mr. Chambers was saying. I think it was about Surrealism. My brain felt surreal right now.

When the lecture was over, I desperately dug around for some gum. All I tasted was the nachos I'd had at lunch. Tom was sketching, and I was lost. I finally found one piece at the bottom of my purse. I blew off the dirt and dust. I took a chance and put it into my mouth. It was a little stale but just fine. I walked up to Mr. Chambers to ask for some art paper.

"Tierney, I'm disappointed in you lately," he said immediately. "You were always such a good student, but lately you've been tardy or spaced out more than usual. I know you have a lot on your plate, but please focus better."

"Sorry," I said.

"I know your friend just passed away, but ever since Tom's arrival, I've seen a slide in your performance here. I hope he's not the cause," he said quietly to me. I gazed over to Tom.

"No, he's not the cause. I'll do better," I said, innocently. "Sorry for being late today, again."

"Okay. I want you to take this class seriously. I understand it's an elective course, and I'm very easy going, maybe too lenient. But I don't like to be taken advantage of."

"I won't. I'll improve," I said, waiting for the right moment to leave.

"Next time you or Tom are late, I'll have no choice but to give extra assignments. Okay?"

"Okay," I replied. I gave him a small smile and returned to my seat.

After I sat down, I felt extremely exhausted. I was carrying so much emotional baggage. I was hoping the rest of the day would go by fast.

"What did he say to you? Was he pissed?" Tom asked.

"Yeah. He said next time we'll have extra assignments."

"Oh."

***

Tom drove me home, and I invited him into the house, in an effort to be normal again. I worked on some homework that I needed to catch up on, and Tom looked through my music. He found the mix CD that he'd made for me.

"Have you listened to this yet?" he asked.

"Don't be mad, I haven't yet, sorry," I said.

"Can I put it on now?"

"Yeah, sure, that would be really good."

He put it into my computer disk drive and relaxed on my bed. I took his lead and settled next to him. I waited and the first song was *Champagne Supernova*, by Oasis. I wasn't sure how Jeremy had felt about this song, but it made me nostalgic for him. Tears came down my face, and Tom sat up slightly above me. He gave me a smile.

"It's okay to cry," he said, sounding like a therapist.

"I know," I said, wiping them across my face.

He gave me a sweet kiss on my mournful eyes. "I love this track."

"I love you," he said.

"I love you, too. I'm sorry for being so…"

"Why are you apologizing? Your best friend just died."

"Yeah," I said sadly.

Suddenly a jazzy bass and piano played behind a melancholy voice.

"I know this, but I can't remember. Who is this?"

"It's *My Funny Valentine* from Chet Baker."

"You really know all the gloomy ones," I said smiling.

"It's supposed to be romantic."

"It is, you have good taste in music," I told him, and we kissed again, longer.

We heard Cat Power's version of *Sea of Love*, and suddenly I was drawn to find a Faulkner book that Jeremy had left at my house months ago. I jumped up, scouring my shelves.

"What are you doing?" Tom asked, puzzled.

"I'm looking for something." I couldn't see it, but I found another book that Jeremy had given me for my birthday last year that I'd forgotten about. I dropped it on my desk, and looked a little frantically in my closet for other Jeremy items.

Tom's eyes watched me explore all the dusty dark regions of my bedroom that had been forgotten. I found a stuffed beanie baby from an ancient birthday that Jeremy had brought to school with a helium balloon, two twelve inch import records, a *Sound of Music* soundtrack CD, ticket stubs to our first concert together, an overdue library book, a dirty Gap T-shirt, and an amethyst crystal from Jeremy's New Age phase. I placed them on my desk, and Tom sensed their importance.

"Hey, what's this?" he asked putting the Minnie Mouse ears on my head.

"I don't know where they came from?"

"They were on the other side of the bed," he said.

"No, I mean I don't even know how I got them. I woke up wearing them, the night we all did ecstasy."

"Jeremy gave them to you. He said he'd gotten them from Disneyland and gave them to you that night." Tom explained. "He wanted to give me Mickey Mouse ears to match, but I wouldn't let him."

"I don't remember. I think Maya told me we played Truth or Dare, but I have no recollection."

"It's probably better that way," he said, coldly.

"Why? She said you were mean or something."

"Me?" he said, sharply. "Your friend wanted me to kiss Gabe."

"They were out of it. I'm sure it was just a joke," I said, slightly affronted.

"Yeah, a joke on me. I didn't appreciate it."

I looked at myself in the mirror, wearing the souvenir from that fateful day. I was numb again. My mom knocked on my open door, startling me. I quickly took the ears off.

"How's it going?" she asked.

"It's going fine," I said wiping my face for any residual tears.

"Do you want to stay for dinner, Tom?" Mom asked.

"Thanks, but my grandmother's expecting me. Maybe another night?" he said, with his usual charm.

"Okay," Mom said, looking like she wanted to say more, but she left.

I looked at my Jeremy pile, holding one piece at a time. I picked up the ticket stub to Coldplay a few years ago at the El Rey. I remembered Jeremy's mom driving us. We were so young. I was in my own nostalgic world.

"Remember this one?" Tom asked, tapping me gently.

"What?" I asked, dazed.

"This song?"

I let the outside world in. It was *Tonight*, from Lykke Li.

"You played it after the Griffith Observatory," he said, putting his arms around me. I stood there listening.

"It reminds me of J," I said crying. "Is it…?" I looked at Tom. "I just want to be alone."

"Okay," Tom said, flatly. "Call me later?"

"I will."

He kissed my cheek and walked out. I heard him say goodbye to my mom at the front door.

***

I pushed around my dinner with my fork, while my mom lectured me about needing sustenance. I put food into my mouth to please her.

"Also, Tierney, your dad and I talked about the trip," she said. "We'll go to the funeral as a family. We've known Jeremy since you were kids."

I looked up at them with dread in my eyes.

"What about your trip? I'll be fine if you go. Seriously," I said.

"We'll leave on a later flight Saturday, after the funeral," Dad said.

"I'll be fine," I said, sincerely.

"It's an important trip that can't be rescheduled," he continued. "That's the only reason for not canceling."

"We want Maya or Tracey to stay over here, or you can go to their houses," Mom said.

"Yeah, I will," I lied.

"It'll be good to have some company," she said.

"You're right," I said.

They looked at each other and smiled at me.

"The way you're feeling is natural," Mom said.

"I know," I said.

"If you want to talk or anything, we're here for you," she said. "But it will take time, and you'll never really be your old self again after an experience like this."

"Did anyone die when you were a teenager?" I asked.

"No," she said quickly.

"My grandfather passed away when I was about your age," Dad said. "But he lived a long and full life. This is different. It's especially hard when someone so young passes."

"He was my oldest friend," I said. "It's weird to think he's gone forever."

"Maybe you'll feel some closure at the funeral," my mom said.

"A funeral seems like some trivial event for the living, not for Jeremy."

"You can do something yourself, something personal," said Dad.

"I guess so," I said. "Maybe I'll write him a letter."

"That's a wonderful idea. I think he would like that," Mom said.

12

I was wearing my mask of sanity the day of the funeral. I felt sick. Everything was foggy and indistinct. Like a robot, I put on a black blouse and skirt, appropriately from my goth period, and I was transported to the funeral home. My parents talked with Maya and Jeremy's parents. Tom, with his grandparents, greeted us.

I had a rock inside my stomach. The casket was closed, thank God – although a part of me longed to see Jeremy again, even like this, one last time. The pastor from the hospital talked about another Jeremy than the one I knew, and Christian fairytales. Jeremy's parents spoke and cried. There were kids and teachers from school whom I recognized, and there were people I had never seen before.

I awakened when Maya and I took the podium. She broke down and left me stranded. My cottony mouth didn't work at first. All the sad blank faces waited for me to speak.

I read from notes I wrote the night before. I tried not to think or look at anyone. I blurted out my words.

"I've known Jeremy since we were eight in elementary school," I said. "He is my oldest friend, and now he's gone. I want to remember him for his laugh, his smile, and the way he always said it like it was. I love him, and I will never forget him."

I stumbled away, hugging Maya. Tears were hot on my face and I could barely see. I think Tracey appeared. I found my parents, and sunk into them.

Next thing I knew, we were in the warm sunshine with the smell of freshly mown grass and newly dug earth. The polished wood casket with Jeremy inside shone in the sun as it was lowered into the ground. Someone handed me a white lily, and I dropped it into the grave. Almost immediately, men shoveled dirt on top, burying his body for eternity.

***

Still pretending to cope, I said goodbye to my parents at home. They drove away in my dad's car, and I gave them a fake smile and waved from the front door. As soon as they left, I slammed the door and hid in my bedroom.

A heavy weight pressed on top of me so hard that I could hardly breathe. Everything was spinning. I woke up when the sun has set, and I texted Tom to come over.

I opened the door crying, wearing the same funeral clothes. He held me tight, and silently I took him to my bedroom. He knew what I wanted, what I needed. He wiped my tears away as we sat on my bed. He unbuttoned my black blouse and I took off his T-shirt.

He kissed me. His smell and his taste were intoxicating. His naked body was warm against mine. Any doubts I might have had about what we were doing seemed insignificant now. His tender embrace electrified my body. I caressed his back downwards over his smooth skin. My heart was pounding, and our kisses became hungrier.

I heard the unzipping of his jeans like some distant thing, and I tugged off my skirt. I climbed on top of him. I wanted him so badly. He gave me a gentle loving smile, and his dark eyes looked into mine. We playfully bit each other. His skin tasted salty. Then he was on top of me and I held my breath as he slipped inside me.

I exhaled, feeling a slight discomfort before our bodies grew accustomed to the virgin sensations. He kissed my body as I gripped him with my legs. I clawed into his thighs as he grasped my shoulders. I moaned away my grief and my pain, and my soul exploded with pleasure.

I felt real again, and we lived together like this on our island for the next couple of days. All the awkwardness and doubt were gone. I was happy being with Tom. We ate naked in the kitchen. We laid in bed all day, with condom wrappers scattered about like fallen fruit.

13

After school Tuesday, Tom bragged to me about his famous grilled cheese sandwiches. Smells of toasty cheesy goodness emanated from our George Foreman Grill. My cell phone rang. It was Tracey. I had been avoiding all calls and any technologically processed messages since Jeremy's funeral. But with my braver self, I could handle anything.

"Hello," I answered.

"Tierney, I finally got hold of you," Tracey said. "I've wanted to hang with you so badly... I'm going back to New York soon."

"Sorry I know, I've been...," I said, watching Tom gather plates, napkins, and juice.

"It's been awful, and Maya is a total mess. How are you doing?" she asked.

"Much better. It's been really crazy."

"I still can't believe that he's not here anymore."

"Yeah," I said, feeling sad. "Tom's really been great keeping me sane." He turned to smile and handed me a plate of grilled cheese neatly cut in two. I smiled back and put it on the table.

"I should go, Tom just made us food," I said.

"He's there now?" she said, her voice sounding suddenly different. "Oh, God, I never told you what I heard about him, did I?" she said.

"It's not important. I don't care," I said, looking at Tom.

"I think you'll care when you hear this," she said, severely.

"Really?" I asked.

"When he was a freshman at a school in New York, he got kicked out for fighting."

"So?"

"What I heard was that they couldn't stop him. The other guy nearly died. For real! It was so bad," Tracey said.

"Oh," I said, puzzled. "Well it doesn't…"

"There's more," she said.

"Okay," I said, turning away from Tom, who looked bored by my phone call.

"I know he's there with you right now, but I feel like I have to tell you this as my friend," she said, with extreme seriousness.

"What is it?" I asked, starting to get freaked out.

"At his last school, he got kicked out for date-raping a girl."

"I don't... I don't know what to say," I told her, confused. I couldn't look at him.

"My boyfriend's best friend, Paul Brent, who's a very reliable source, went to Columbus with Tom. He knew the girl. He told me that Tom drugged her with sleeping pills. She told the school, and they kept it all hush from the police if his parents agreed to have him leave," Tracey explained.

"What?" I exclaimed, feeling hot and sweaty.

"I care about you, Tierney. This is why I'm telling you this. Be really, really careful with him."

"Okay," I said.

"Paul wouldn't make this stuff up. He's a good guy," she said.

"What should I...?" I stuttered, wanting the call to end and never have happened. "I'll get to the bottom of this. Don't worry about..."

"Okay, Tierney. Please call me back so I can see you. Take care and please, please keep in touch. I miss you."

"Of course. I miss you, too. Goodbye," I said.

I faced the unsuspecting Tom, who was eating his gooey sandwich.

"You should eat it while it's still hot," he said, with his mouth full.

"Did you get kicked out of school?" I asked plainly.

"What are you talking about?" he said, puzzled.

"A really good friend of mine, who flew back from New York for the funeral, just told me some stuff."

"What stuff?" he said. "You can't believe the gossip people spread around. Everybody has their own agenda."

"She was serious, Tom. She was worried about me. I trust her, she wouldn't make trouble for me unless it meant something, especially now. And it was bad, Tom. Not just rumors. She said it's from a source she trusts absolutely."

He was silent for a long moment, then suddenly he turned on me.

"My ex-girlfriend is a lying bitch!" he yelled, with a dark gleam I had never seen before in his eyes.

"That's not the answer I was looking for," I said solemnly.

"What did you hear? That I raped a girl?" he asked, almost mockingly.

"Tracey wouldn't lie to me, and she's not a gossip," I said.

"I did not rape anyone!" he shouted, red-faced.

"She said that you drugged the girl with sleeping pills," I said, trying to stay calm and keep control of the situation.

"My ex-girlfriend wanted to ruin my life. She went to my school and told them all these lies to save herself… I don't know."

"Why?"

"Her parents are hardcore Catholic," he said angrily, pacing the kitchen. "They found out we had sex and …"

"Why would she lie?" I asked.

"She's insane! Are you happy now? You got the dirt on me!" he shouted.

"Is that why you moved here?" I asked calmly.

"No, my parents really did hate each other and really got divorced. My dad screwed Mom over, so we couldn't afford to stay in New York," he said bitterly. "Is this what you want, the truth?"

"I just wanted to hear your side of the story," I said, directly.

"The truth is, I've been Mr. Nice-Guy too long for the death of your druggie best friend..." he continued.

"What? Who are you?" I yelled back, stunned. "Did you just act good to get into my pants? Is this what you're saying?"

"No, but..."

"But what?" I asked.

"But you and your friends are shallow and narcissistic..."

"What?" I demanded.

"You guys just want to have a good time all the time, and you don't care about anything else. Your lives have no meaning," he said, with threatening eyes.

"You don't know me that well," I shouted. "You have no right to say that to me!"

"Your friend deserved to die," Tom said. "He was really fucked up, in every way possible."

"Get out of here now!" I screamed, hurling the now-soggy grilled cheese at him. It landed on his sleeve, and he furiously tossed it to the floor.

He seized me just below my shoulders with his talon-like hands.

"I love you!" he pleaded.

"Are you going to hurt me like that boy in freshman year?" I howled.

He dropped his hands swiftly. "What, your friend told you that too?" He turned away. "She's got a big mouth. Are you satisfied? Now you know all my dirty secrets!"

He looked at me, and I stared at him with searing animosity. He knew there was no point in further discussion, and he left suddenly out of the front door without bothering to shut it.

I stood in the kitchen, hot tears streaming down, watching his black pickup truck screech out of our driveway. I held my face in my hands and cried out my rage.

***

Tracey came over as soon as I called her. I cried into her arms when I told her about our fight.

"Did you break up then?" she asked.

"I don't know. I guess so," I said. "I'm not sure if I'm sad or just really angry with him. I don't know who he is anymore."

"Let's do something to get your mind off it."

"Like thinking about Jeremy?" I said.

"No, I don't know. Something else," Tracey said.

"Do you really think he raped a girl?" I asked her.

"It sounds awful," she said. "But Paul wouldn't lie. And there's the other stuff, about the fight with the boy. He gave him a real beating, like seriously bad. How did he react when you told him?"

"He freaked," I said. "He totally freaked. He was like someone I didn't know anymore."

Tracey hugged me hard, then we went into my room and played some music really loud, trying to get our minds off everything that had happened.

After what might have been an hour or more, I checked my computer, where there were tons of emails waiting for me. While Tracey sat on my bed and watched me, I read through and deleted everything, without glancing at more than the headers. They were mostly words of condolence about Jeremy. Then I found something from Jack.

"Hey, Tracey, I have an email from someone I met in Carmel with my parents."

"Who?" she asked, looking up from a trashy magazine she had found.

"I don't think I told you. I met this college guy who showed me the stars one night."

"Wait, you had a date with another boy? You didn't tell me that," she said.

"It wasn't a date. He's an astronomy major at Berkeley. He was showing me the constellations."

"Were your parents with you?"

"No."

"You two were alone?" she asked.

"Yes."

"Watching the heavenly bodies alone with someone of the opposite sex is a date," she said, smiling.

"It was platonic."

"You can never just be friends with a guy unless he's gay," she said.

"Why not?"

"There's sexual tension or the probability of a hookup. That's just the way it is."

"Whatever."

I read his email, and it was the U.F.O. video he'd promised to send me. I uploaded the mpeg file.

"Come over here. Let's watch this."

"What is it? A love letter?"

"No, silly. He told me he had footage of a real-life U.F.O."

"No way. He's crazy, too!" Tracey exclaimed, jumping onto my bed behind me for a better view.

"Shut up. Let me play it," I said, relieved to have a distraction from Tom.

We waited for the video to play.

"I'm so excited! I've never seen a flying saucer before!" she shouted.

It was a bright cloudless daytime California sky. We heard lots of wind, and I couldn't make out any spacecraft. I saw palm trees to one side of the frame and a large hillside with houses scattered about, and we heard humorous dialogue.

"*Oh wow, there it is,*" Jack said in the background.

"*Where is it?*" An older man said on the video.

"*I want to see,*" a young girl whined off screen.

"Where is it?" Tracey asked.

"I don't know. I don't see anything," I said.

I enlarged the video so it was full screen. I scanned the sky and saw a speck of silver-white.

"Is that it?" I pointed.

"I guess?" Maya said.

"*Is it moving or am I just moving*?" Jack asked, onscreen.

"*It's way too big to be a balloon, and it's static,*" the man said on the video.

"*Now I lost it. Where is it?*" Jack asked.

"*Can I take the picture?*" cried the girl again.

"*My feet are burning. Can you hold the camera wile I get my shoes?*" Jack asked.

"*I can't see it. You shoot it,*" said the man.

"*It's there behind the palm frond,*" Jack said.

"*If it suddenly shoots off to the side, we'll know it's a U.F.O.,*" said the man laughing. "*I can't see it in the viewfinder, you shoot it.*"

"*I'll do it,*" Jack said.

"*Is it still there*?" asked the man.

"*Yeah it's still there,*" Jack said. "*This is amazing.*"

The image became magnified, and we saw an uncanny rotating shiny silver spherical object in the sky.

"That's it!" I pointed to Tracey.

"Oh my God, that's so weird!" she exclaimed.

The video went black. The whole thing was a just a few minutes.

"Their conversation was too funny," she said. "Let's watch it again!"

After a few viewings, we got a better picture of the U.F.O. and Jack's family life.

"I think you had to be there. It was so small onscreen," I said to Tracey.

"Yeah, but it was really cool. When are you going to see him again?" she asked.

"I don't know. I hadn't heard from him until this email."

"Email him back saying you just broke up with your rapist boyfriend and now you're available," Tracey said.

"Shut up. I'm not going to say that."

I went back to Jack's email. I wrote, "*Thanks for the video. Hope all is well. It's been really crazy here. Tell you about it soon. Tierney.*"

"Did you write, '*with love from Tierney?*'"Tracey asked.

I looked up at her, smiling. "No, I didn't."

"Let's call Maya. What is she doing?"

"I don't know. Probably hanging out with Jeremy's mom,"

"Really? What is up with that?"

"It's complicated. They became close after Jeremy was hospitalized. I guess they needed each other."

I called Maya on my cellphone but got her voicemail. I called her house and her mom answered.

"Hi, it's Tierney, is Maya at home?"

"Hi, Tierney. Maya is here but she's packing right now."

"Where is she going?"

"The school called and they suggested she be sent to rehab for her drug problem. Did you know about this?"

"No, I…"

"They found some of her friend, Todd's parent's prescription medication bottles in her purse. I had a long chat with her counselor and the principal."

"What! I didn't know any of this."

"Why don't you come over and say goodbye," her mom said.

"I'll come over now."

***

"We need to visit Maya right now," I told Tracey, urgently. "She's being sent to rehab by the school."

"What do you mean?"

"Her mom just told me that they found some of Todd's parents' meds in her purse."

"Okay, let's go now, poor girl. She's dealing with so much," Tracey said, worried. "I'm glad I moved east. These guys around here, they're all drugs or psycho."

"This is serious, Tracey."

***

Maya's mom allowed us thirty minutes with Maya in her room if the door remained open.

Maya was busy packing her clothes into a small suitcase.

"What happened?" I asked.

"I was sent to my counselor's office and she checked my bag with the principal there," she began. "I seriously had no idea that those drugs were in my bag," she explained.

"What was it?" Tracey asked.

"I don't know, Xanax and Valium, I think," Maya said. "I said that someone put them in there. They immediately gave me a drug test and called my parents."

"What happened with the test?" I asked. "Were you clean?"

"That was part of the problem," Maya admitted. "I guess Todd and I had been kind of out of control since what happened to J, and the horrible thing with our baby. But I don't believe Todd would do this to me. Why? He's not that fucked up."

"Your mom didn't seem too thrilled," I said.

"Yeah, she's pissed," Maya said. "I told her that I didn't think Todd would sell me out like that. But she hates him now."

"What's going to happen to him?" Tracey asked.

"He's going to another rehab center," Maya said. "But in a way, I don't mind getting a break from here."

"Where is it? Can we visit you?" I asked.

"I'm not sure. I don't think you can visit. I'll just be gone for thirty days," Maya said. Tracey and I hugged her.

"Why did all this have to happen to Jeremy?" I said, crying.

"I'm so sorry, Tierney," Maya replied, crying too. "I didn't... I wasn't thinking. I called as soon as I realized. You know how he sleeps and sleeps."

"What are you talking about? I don't blame you at all. I know you did everything. If it wasn't for you, it could have been worse," I said.

"How much worse? He died!" She cried harder. We hugged each other and wept. It felt better to let it all out.

"Let's not have a cry fest," Tracey said, laughing through her own tears. "I loved what you said at the funeral."

Maya nodded, trying to dry her tears.

"It was so short. I didn't know what to say," I replied.

"It was perfect and simple. I'm sorry I bailed on you," Maya said.

"It was Jeremy's funeral. It was hard on everyone. But don't blame yourself. It was a mistake, and he was always teetering on the edge."

"Yeah, I guess so."

"You know what really pisses me off?" I asked her.

"What?"

"Tom told me that we were shallow, and our lives were meaningless." "What is he doing that is so wonderful and thought provoking?" Maya asked.

"I don't know, beating someone up? And I had just slept with him over the weekend," I said, staring at a red-eyed Maya.

"You didn't mention that!" Maya exclaimed. "How was it?"

"It was so amazing, but now I feel dirty after finding out about him. It's confusing," I whispered.

"Sex is fun. I wish I were having sex with someone cool..." Maya said quietly.

"Maybe all the gossip is wrong? Maybe he's an okay guy," I said to Tracey.

"Are you going to give him another chance?" asked Tracey. "Be really careful, Tierney."

"I don't know. He was scary in our fight. He was a completely different person. He's a stranger to me."

"He was always a bit aloof," Maya said.

"You know what?" I asked. "He said Jeremy deserved to die."

"What! How dare he? Who does he think he is?" Maya screamed. "You shouldn't get back together with him, Tierney."

"I didn't really think I was going to. I know it's over. It would never be the same," I admitted.

"I can't believe he had the nerve to say that!" Maya exclaimed.

"I know," I said, mind-numbed again.

"Didn't I give this to you ages ago, and you still have it?" Tracey pointed to something in the closet.

Maya grabbed a box and put it on her bed. "Yeah, but I don't think I've used it for a while."

"I vaguely recall using it with you guys and Jeremy when we were really stoned," I said.

"We were always stoned," Tracey laughed.

"You should take it, Tierney," Maya said, giving me the Ouija Board box. "You can use it while I'm in lock down. Ask the spirits if I'll be saved."

"Okay, why not?" I said.

"Hey, this stuff works for me, let's use it later," said Tracey.

In the kitchen, we heard the telephone ring. Maya's mom was having a serious conversation, and we heard her talking about Maya's predicament. We were quiet, trying to listen to who it was.

14

"Stephanie has Jeremy's toxicology report, and she wants you to come over this minute," Maya's mom told us a few minutes later, after she hung up the phone. "You can go quickly, but come straight back. She sounded concerned, and I know how important he was to you."

"Thank you mom, we'll come right back, I promise," Maya said.

***

We drove in silence to Jeremy's house. I hadn't been there since Maya's miscarriage. I immediately saw his red Audi station wagon in the driveway, like a stop sign for his existence. Maya, Tracey, and I couldn't keep our eyes off it as we walked to the front door.

Jeremy's mom, Stephanie, quickly ushered us through the door with bleary eyes. She looked glamorous even in her yoga pants, and the house was immaculate. The door to Jeremy's room was a menacing presence as we sat in the living room. I sensed that he was in there taking a nap, and if I waited long enough, he would wake up and greet us.

Memories of drugs and merriment flooded my mind as we sat. Maya and Jeremy would be fighting over music, while I took another hit of something. But now the windows were all closed, leaving the house stale and airless. Stephanie and Maya still had their special relationship, and they chatted like sorority sisters. Tracey and I just gazed at them.

"I'm so glad you came over so quickly, Maya," she said, then looking at all of us, "and Tierney and Tracey. I just got the final toxicology report from the hospital. I thought you would want to be the first to know."

"Thanks. We're so grateful that you treat us like family," Maya said.

"You are family, especially to Jeremy after the divorce. I feel like everything is my fault for leaving his father. Maybe if we had stayed together, he would still be here?" she said tearily.

"No, you left for a reason," Maya said, sounding suddenly more like the adult here. "Your marriage was falling apart. I'm sure it was better for Jeremy to be in an environment where there wasn't yelling and fighting all the time."

Jeremy's mom pulled out some documents from underneath a paperweight. I held my breath, waiting in anticipation. She looked at the papers and then back at us. Maya, Tracey, and I felt the mounting tension.

"Jeremy died from an overdose of sedatives," his mother began, falteringly. "He took one Xanax and two Ambien, and there were trace amounts of MDMA and marijuana in his blood, also."

"Ambien?" I asked.

"Yes," she looked at me intensely. "I don't know where he got that from. I had every other kind of sleeping pill, and numerous other medications, because of my various conditions. But I didn't even know he took anything to sleep, besides the occasional smoke."

"I don't remember him taking it that night, either," Maya said, with a serious look on her face. "I know he gave me a Xanax to help me sleep. After I took it, I was out straight away. We should ask Tom."

"That's right, Tom was there. I forgot about that," I said, suddenly thinking that this might mean something. I could be wrong, but when I looked over at Maya and she looked back at me with obviously the same thought knocking around her brain, I started to get a sick feeling in my stomach.

"Also, I reread the police report," Jeremy's mother went on. "At the time, everything was happening so fast that I barely absorbed anything. It states that Jeremy had bruises all over his body. They were minor, but do you know if he fell down that day, either of you?" she asked.

"Bruises?" Maya asked, puzzled. "I don't know anything about that."

I was hot with anger thinking about Tom. What had he done

to Jeremy?

"That's really strange," I said quietly.

"I know. I suppose it doesn't matter now," Jeremy's mother

said, sadly. "They weren't the cause of death. Maybe he tripped

over something at school or I don't know what during the day?"

"Maybe?" I said, unconvinced.

"I'm going away soon," Stephanie said. "I've been going

back to yoga classes, and they have a retreat in India. I'll be able

to detox myself. I know I've been a mess but I've thrown away all

my drugs and I'm leaving in a few weeks."

"That will be perfect for you," Maya said, smiling. "Kind of

like my retreat, but you can't drink the water."

Stephanie hugged Maya. "I'm so glad you understand.

You'll be fine in rehab. Your mom said they would have

bereavement counseling especially for you. It will be good for you,

for both of us."

"I know," Maya, said, with tears running down her face. "Don't worry, I'll be back before you, and we'll never forget Jeremy, any of us."

***

We walked out of the house in a confused and angry state. There were more questions than answers in the toxicology report. I stared at the bright blue sky, looking for an U.F.O. I could hear Jack's happy voice in my mind, videotaping the spherical object in the sky that afternoon so far away from where we were now.

We passed my house on the way back to Maya's place and Tom was in his truck waiting for me in my driveway. Maya shot out of the car before we finished parking. I tried to catch up. Like a madwoman, she yelled at him through his window.

"What did you do to Jeremy?" she screamed.

"I didn't do anything. Control yourself," he said, annoyed.

"Did you give him any of your sleeping pills?" I demanded.

"Yes, but he asked for them," Tom said flatly. "Why?"

"He died from an overdose of sleeping pills!" Maya shouted.

I stood behind her, pulling her away. She tried to open his door, looking like she wanted to hit him.

"I didn't cram them down his throat," Tom yelled back. "He asked for two and I gave them to him."

"You killed him!" Maya had tears pouring down her face now.

"It was going to happen sooner or later, the way he inhaled any drugs he could lay his hands on," Tom continued cruelly.

"I want you to leave now," I said firmly.

"I just wanted to talk to you, Tierney," he said, clearly thinking that he had a chance of repairing our relationship. He started to get out of his truck.

"Why did Jeremy have bruises all over his body?" Maya screamed at him.

"What?" he asked. "How should I know?"

"I hate you! He would still be here if we'd never met you!" Maya shrieked.

She started shoving and punching him. He pushed her away so hard that she fell to the ground.

"You dick. It was all your fault!" Tracey yelled, helping Maya.

"You crazy bitch! Get off me!" he said.

I helped Tracey get Maya back on her feet. "Just go!" I shouted at Tom.

"Come on, Tierney. I was defending myself. I want to talk to you, just the two of us," he begged me.

"Leave us alone!" I told him.

I planted myself between him and Maya and Tracey, and gave him an unforgiving glare.

He climbed back in his truck and drove away with a loud squeal of his tires. We watched him leave, and I held Maya, who was shaking in Tracey's arms, crying.

"I can't believe him," Maya said.

"Yeah and I slept with him," I said. "Come on, we'll take you home."

Tracey and I said a final goodbye to Maya, and her mom saw us to the door.

"Thanks for taking care of my Maya," she said.

"Maya is a good girl," I said.

"I know," she said. "This has been such a hard time for everybody. Jeremy in the hospital, then his passing, especially like that. It took its toll on her. I think going away for a month will do her good." Maya's mom glanced back at her daughter with obvious love.

"I don't think it was Todd's fault about the medication in her purse," I said.

"No, it wasn't him. The school said it was another boy," her mom replied quietly. "But I'm letting her think it was Todd. He's no good for her. I hope this will finally end it with him. I'm afraid one day she'll tell me she's pregnant with his baby."

"That's a good idea," I said, instantly curious and definitely not wanting to dwell on a Maya pregnancy. "Who was the boy?" I asked.

"They wouldn't say, but I think it's for the best. The clinic is going to focus on counseling for her. Thanks, girls," she said, subtly ushering us out and closing the door quickly.

***

"I miss him still," Tracey said, as we slumped on my
bedroom floor.

"I don't think that ever goes away," I replied.

"I can't believe…Tom was so nasty. Really vicious."

"I know. I told you. He's another person. I don't know who
he is anymore."

"I'm going to get the Ouija board and get some
explanations," Tracey said.

She climbed over to the box near her bag and brought it to
me. She opened up the gently worn board and placed the triangle
piece on top.

"Do you have any candles?" she asked.

"Yeah, I guess. Does that help?"

"I'm not sure. But it helps create the right mood or
ambiance."

"What is that thing called?" I asked.

"The planchette? It helps the spirit direct our fingers to the
right letters or numbers or responses," she said.

My head was still reeling from our afternoon with Maya and Tom, and already the whole séance scene was becoming too bizarre. I found some beeswax candles I had made in junior high and lit them around us. Tracey, completely genuinely, moved the triangular planchette over the board. Her slender fingers gently moved the piece everywhere.

"Are you moving it?" I asked.

"Yes, I'm just getting the feel of the spiritual room right now," she answered, sincerely.

"Um, is this going to work? Are you asking for Jeremy's spirit to help you?"

"Well, his would be perfect, but I think it's really any nearby spirit that will help guide us."

"Why would they help us rather than point us in the wrong direction?" "They're lost souls. They help us so we can help them," she said.

"How do we help them?"

"I think sometimes we can lead them to the light and they can go to heaven."

"Heaven?"

"Or the other way."

"You believe that, Tracey?"

"I don't know. I guess so," she said. "All I know is this thing has worked for me in the past. Let's just try it now. It won't hurt."

"Okay. Let's give it a go," I said.

"Help me by gently placing the tips of your fingers on the other side on mine here," she said, pointing to the planchette.

I did what she told me, and I kneeled next to her.

"Spirits, please help us, we beg you. Can you hear me?" she asked, in a steady, quiet voice.

I didn't know what to expect, but I felt a tug at my fingers. The pointer device slowly moved to the word, "*Yes.*"

"Did you move that, Tracey?" I asked.

"No, the lost soul in the room did," she said, trancelike.

My mind was a little spaced – and the Ouija was spooking me.

"Thank you for your help. Who are you?" she asked. "Or what were you?"

We waited and stared at the board. I looked at Tracey, who was concentrating really hard. She closed her eyes, and I did the same. Again, the piece at our fingertips crept to the middle and stopped. We opened our eyes, and it had landed on the letter, "G." It then went to "I" and "R."

"Are you moving it, Tierney?" Tracey asked.

"No way, are you?"

"It's not me," she said, with eyes that seemed unusually bright all of a sudden, but also a little fearful.

The planchette finally stopped at, "L."

"The ghost is a girl."

"I can read it, but I don't believe this. It's scaring me. I don't think I want to use it anymore," I said.

"I'll just ask it one question we're dying to know the answer to. Okay?" Tracey asked me.

"Okay."

"Who killed Jeremy?" she said starkly, staring at me. I was nervous for what would happen next.

We waited for what seemed like an eternity before the planchette moved. It went in circles, not landing on any particular place. My heart was racing and my hands felt sweaty.

"Was it accidental?" I asked quietly.

The piece moved faster in circles, looping around the board.

"Are you moving it, Tracey?"

"I told you, it's not me. It's the girl spirit in the room," she said.

I looked around the room for anything unusual. It was just my room. Everything was in its place and the candles were burning like any other candles. Suddenly, Tracey shrieked loudly and started to cry.

"Look!" she shouted.

The piece we'd been holding onto was pointing to, "*NO.*"

"Jeremy's death was not accidental?" I asked.

The piece moved around the board and landed on "*NO*" again. My heart felt like it was going to explode. Tracey cried, and I was trying to get my thoughts together.

"Did he do it?" she yelled out.

I rubbed my hands together before placing them back on the planchette. I was surprised at how cold they felt. Tracey looked at me with red teary eyes. We waited for movement, and nothing happened. I watched her for guidance.

"Please tell us, we need to know. You have been so helpful. Maybe we can help you too?" she pleaded.

The piece slowly moved, but without direction. Gradually it stopped on, "*FAREWELL.*"

"No! No! The spirit is going away. Please help us," Tracey said, crying harder.

I let go of the piece and sat up straight.

"Does it usually work like that?" I asked softly.

"No. That was amazing. It's never worked like that before," she admitted, shaking her head. "Sorry, I feel drained."

We slumped on pillows on the rug, deep in our own thoughts.

"I'm going to get some water. Want anything?" I asked.

"No, I'm good," she said.

***

Slowly I drank my glass of water and found myself obsessing, cleaning the kitchen. I put away the George Foreman Grill, and I wiped away bits of cheese from the floor, from what felt like a different life, almost as far away as before Jeremy died. I was in a total daze. By the time I made my way back to my bedroom, Tracey was asleep, curled up in my bed with my comforter. The candles were still burning.

I started straightening up the clutter, when suddenly I looked at the Ouija board. I had an idea. I knelt down on the floor where we'd left it. I took the planchette with my fingertips, and I asked.

"Jeremy, if you can hear me, why did Tom do it?"

The heart-shaped piece was still for the longest time. I was about to let go, then slowly it started to glide about the board.

It circled and circled all the letters, as if it couldn't quite decide. Then it went to the letter, "R," and then "A." I was puzzled by this – but excited by the planchette actually moving on its own.

It began to move faster, and finally landed on "P." Then it stopped on another letter, which totally freaked me out.

"What?" I asked. Tracey stirred a little on my bed but didn't wake.

"Who?" I asked quietly.

The Ouija board piece swirled all over the board. I was barely touching it. It spelled, "T," "I," "E," "R," "N," "E," "Y." I gasped. I was shaking so hard that my teeth were rattling. The lit candle starting flickering and went out when a gust of cold air blew past me. I breathed in my anger and gained a new confidence.

"Thank you. I'll talk to you again soon," I said calmly.

I found my cell phone in my purse and texted Tom.

> **Tierney: Meet me at the Santa Monica Pier**

I changed my clothes and glanced at myself in my closet mirror. I put on my "T" heart necklace that Tom had given me, and his old hoodie, too.

15

We're back at the pier. It's night. The Ferris Wheel is behind us, and the Mexican restaurant, too. Tom has followed me down the three steps that lead to the farthest deck. We're alone. He stares at me with that pitiful mix of desire and longing – and fear, I think. I'd like to think he's at least a little afraid of what I may know now.

"Which sleeping pill do you take?" I ask him.

"Um, I take Restoril," he says. "Why?"

"Restoril?" I say, confused.

"I just started it a few days ago. I was on Ambien for years. It wasn't working for me anymore."

"Oh, Ambien," I say, rehearsing in my mind the pills that Jeremy had in his system when he died.

"Honestly, what happened that night we did the ecstasy?" I ask. "You know I can't remember. Did you have something to do with my not remembering?"

"That's a strange question," he says.

"Did you?"

He stares at me, as a wave breaks fiercely on one of the caissons below us.

"Tierney we don't need to go over this. You know I care deeply for you."

"You gave me Ambien didn't you," I say, caressing his face with my hand. "I've slept with you. You can tell me the truth." His hard eyes look sadly into mine.

"But I fell in love with you."

"I thought I did, too," I tell him.

He watches me play delicately with the pendant he gave me. He moves closer.

"It was so easy. You and your friends would swallow, smoke and probably snort anything."

"And you wanted to take advantage of me?" I say, calmly.

"You gave me that ecstasy. I was turned on and I just wanted to seal the deal – but your friend, Jeremy, walked in on us."

"Where?"

"We were in his mom's room, I think, and he was really pissed off with me. Suddenly he was all Mr. Protective. He got Gabe to drive you straight home."

"But you were trying to rape me?" I say. "Why did you do that? I thought...I thought we were special."

"Like I said, it was too easy. You were such a tease. I was trying to handle you," Tom says, gripping my waist tightly now.

"Did you force the pills on Jeremy, too?" I ask.

"Can I just have one kiss?" he says. "You smell so sweet. For old time's sake?"

"Maybe, just tell me what you did," I say, grabbing his chin with my hand.

I give him my best smile. "Please tell me, Tom."

"Okay, for a kiss."

"Fine, just one." I close in on him with my lips hovering just over his. "But tell me first, I ask politely. *Ladies first*," I whisper.

"You are too much of a tease," he says. He pulls me to him, angry now, forcing his lips onto mine. His hands are on the back of my head, pushing it into his face. Then he shoves me down onto the railing. I'm shocked by his rage, but I pretend it's all fun and games. I laugh gently.

"You're not playing fair. Now please tell me, Tom."

"I had to slap him a little, but not much. Jeremy enjoyed it. I should have given him more, the little fag. But I didn't really want to kill him. Just give him a lesson in interfering. Him dying was just a happy accident," Tom says, his face a scary mask.

He grabs me again, roughly. He starts kissing my neck and grazing it with his teeth.

"I want less talk and more action," he says. "I deserve it now. After being your kiss-ass, perfect boyfriend. Let's have one more little poke," he says, evilly.

He grips the front of my jeans with one hand, while the other is clutching my neck. I realize I need to get away *now!* I bite his finger nearest my mouth and push him with everything I have.

"*Ow!* You bitch!" he yells.

"Get off me!"

I fall to the ground near a fire extinguisher and I fumble with its latch. I need it to undo it fast. Tom pulls me back hard and I hold on with dear life.

"You were always the feisty one!" he exclaims.

I nearly have the latch unhooked when he pushes me down. I fall hard, face forward, onto the wooden boards with the fire extinguisher beneath me. Pain shoots into my chest. Tom is trying to get my jeans off from behind. I scream and scream.

"Get off me, you dick! Get off!"

He pulls me by my jeans with brute strength, causing a ripping noise. I'm clutching the fire extinguisher, and I push him as hard as I can. He's laughing at me now. My heart is racing. He grabs my arm, and with everything I have within me, I pound the fire extinguisher into his head. A loud thud of metal on human skull reverberates in the night air, and he falls back, pulling me with him.

Together, we fall into the cold night sea, leaving the fire extinguisher behind on the deck. The frigid water stings me but his grip is immediately released. I'm underwater, and I kick to the surface as he sinks further into the ocean. Moonlight catches the choppy waves.

I pull myself back onto the pier, finding the bloody fire extinguisher lying innocent on the wooden boards. Using my foot, I kick it so it rolls into the ocean. I take off my "T" heart necklace to throw into the sea, but I stop and put it in my pocket instead.

As I run to my car, I remember what Jack said about the moon. We always see the same side of it from Earth. From the beginning of time, every woman, man, child, animal and plant has seen the same side of the moon.

Running through darkness halfway down the pier, I pass a young romantic couple and a few more fishermen. When I reach the brightly lit areas, I see tourists and families. My step is lighter, and my face feels more relaxed, almost as if I'm smiling. I sense a sudden euphoria – a joy – that it is finally over.

I unlock my mom's car – and I realize that Tom's truck was parked next to it. But now it's gone. My chest tightens and I look everywhere for a sign of him. There are some wet footprints, but I'm confused as to whether they are mine or possibly his.

My face is flushed and my heart is pulsating loudly. I'm shaking, and I drive home as fast as I can.

16

At home, I make sure I lock everything. Even though I have to sleep on the floor because Tracey has occupied my bed, I sleep better than I have for a long time. I know I am safe from him here at my own home.

In the morning, I see Tracey off before I drive to school. I decide to keep her in the dark about my meeting with Tom. I don't want to scare her. The day seems to shine on me. After I stop looking over my shoulder for Tom to reappear, I ace my pop math quiz, have lunch with new friends, and then a really successful art critique with Mr. Chambers.

After school, I clean up before my parents are due to arrive home in the evening. I find some nice paper and go outside to our patio to write my farewell letter to Jeremy. I'm nearly finished when my parents find me.

"Hi," I say upon seeing them.

"What are you doing, honey?" asks Mom.

"Writing a letter to Jeremy, like you suggested," I say with a smile.

"Oh, how lovely," she says.

"What did you do while we were gone?" Dad asks.

"Hung out with Tracey. It was good."

"Well, you seem very content, more mature even," says Mom, happily.

"After I write this letter to Jeremy, I'm going to burn it so he'll get it wherever he is, like the Chinese burning money for deceased ancestors in heaven."

"Wow, that's a wonderful idea!" exclaims Dad.

"You really are all grown up," says Mom. "We'll leave you to finish, and I'll order some pizza for dinner."

"Okay, see you back inside," I say.

***

Dear Jeremy,

I miss you so much. I still find it hard to believe that you are no longer here. I always look for you at school and around every corner. I imagine you've reincarnated into an eagle soaring in the sky or a magical pink unicorn. I don't know how these things work ~ perhaps you are somebody's newborn baby?

You are my oldest friend, and we shared so many experiences and secrets that I've never shared with anybody else. Yesterday, we used Maya's old Ouija board to ask about your death and about Tom. I know he's the one who caused your death, and I know what you did for me.

He gave you the Ambien, that much was obvious. I had no idea that he tried to rape me at your house, and you were just being my friend. I will be eternally grateful for what you did. He wanted you dead. He didn't think you deserved to live, and I think he resented you in some way. Who knows what someone deranged like Tom thinks? Even now, the fact that we kissed and that I let him … It sends shivers down my spine.

So I took Tom to the Santa Monica Pier and he tried to hurt me again. I bashed his head with a fire extinguisher. I did that all by myself. I thought it was a great idea. Then we fell into the freezing ocean, where I thought the fish were going to eat his remains. But when I got back to the parking lot, his truck was gone. I don't know how, but I think he's on the run. I do know that one day we'll meet *again and I'll make sure he pays for what he did to*

you.

I hope to send you more letters to stay in

contact with you. Yesterday, I felt your spirit as I

used the Ouija board. Was it really you?

I miss you terribly and I love you forever. Best

Friends Forever and ever and ever. If you can give

me a sign sometime, please do.

Be good and maybe one day we will meet each

other again.

Love, Tierney

***

The sun has set and it's the magic hour. The light is diffused and everything looks mystical. I take the letter to the cactus planters near our pool. Using a lighter Jeremy once left at my house, I light it. The orange flame quickly turns it into rectangular

black ash. Then a breeze captures it, scattering it into a million

pieces.

I whisper, "Goodbye," as I watch it swirl away into the

darkening sky.

***

Based in California, Charong Chow is an internationally exhibited artist, author and mother of two. Her debut novel "Random," was inspired by her best friend's death. A food lover, she writes a recipe and lifestyle blog with her children, www.EatingWithHudson.com. She also writes for various publications when not caring for her family and menagerie of animals.

Made in United States
Troutdale, OR
01/23/2025

28266631R00137